R. D. Bartlett and Patricia P. Bartlett

Iguanas

Everything about Selection, Care, Nutrition,
Diseases, Breeding, and Behavior

With 44 Color Photographs

Illustrations by Michele Earle-Bridges

BARRON'S

All inquiries should be addressed to:
Barron's Educational Series, Inc.
250 Wireless Boulevard
Hauppauge, NY 11788

International Standard Book No. 0-8120-1876-1

Library of Congress Catalog Card No. 94-46720

Library of Congress Cataloging-in-Publication Data

Bartlett, Richard D., 1938–
    Iguanas : everything about purchase, housing, care, nutrition, breeding, and diseases : with a special chapter on understanding iguanas / Richard Bartlett and Patricia Bartlett ; illustrations by Michele Earle-Bridges.
        p.   cm.
    Includes index.
    ISBN 0-8120-1876-1
    1. Iguanas as pets.   I. Bartlett, Patricia Pope, 1949– .   II. Earle-Bridges, Michele. III. Title.
    SF459.I38B37   1995   94-46720
    639.3′95—dc20   CIP

Printed in Hong Kong

678   9955   98765

About the authors

R. D. Bartlett is a herpetologist who has authored more than 350 articles and three books on reptiles. He lectures extensively and has participated in field studies across North and Latin America.

In 1978 he began the Reptilian Breeding and Research Institute (RBRI), a private facility. Since its inception, more than 150 species of reptiles and amphibians have been bred at RBRI, some for the first time in the United States under captive conditions. Successes at the RBRI include several endangered species.

Bartlett is a member of numerous herpetological and conservation organizations.

Patricia Bartlett received her B.S. from Colorado State University and became the editor for an outdoor book publisher in St. Petersburg, Florida. Subsequently, she worked for the science museum in Springfield, Massachusetts and for the historical museum in Ft. Myers, Florida. She is the author of five books on natural history and historical subjects.

Photo Credits

Michele Earle-Bridges: pages 24, 51. All other photographs were taken by R. D. Bartlett.

Photos on the Covers

Front: *Iguana iguana* (juvenile). Inside front: *Sauromalus obesos.* Inside back: *Brachylophus fasciatus.* Back: *Iguana iguana.*

Important Note

Before using any of the electrical equipment described in this book, be sure to read Avoiding Electrical Accidents on page 23.

While handling iguanas you may occasionally receive bites, scratches, or tail blows. If your skin is broken, see your physician immediately.

Some terrarium plants may be harmful to the skin or mucous membranes of human beings. If you notice any signs of irritation, wash the area thoroughly. See your physician if the condition persists.

Iguanas may transmit certain infections to humans. Always wash your hands carefully after handling your specimens. Always supervise children who wish to observe your iguanas.

Contents

Acknowledgments

Thanks are due to Mike Beaver, Mike Ellard, Bill Love, Rob MacInnes, Chris McQuade, and Sheila Rodgers for providing photgraphic opportunities.

Ellen and Bob Nicol shared with me some observations on their own iguanas—lizards which, I am sure, consider themselves a people.

The medication tables in the health section were provided by Richard Funk, D.V.M.

Food values were excerpted from charts first made public by the long defunct International Turtle and Tortoise Society.

I wish to extend special acknowledgment to four individuals for their published contributions on the captive care of green iguanas. Philippe DeVosjoli, Bob Ehrig, Fredric L. Frye, D.V.M., and Florence Gutierrez, D.V.M. Dr. Frye also read the manuscript and provided comments and suggestions that have helped us improve the quality of our presentation.

A wholesaler's holding tank for baby iguanas.

A beautiful, green hatchling iguana dwarfed by a fern-frond.

Preface

Green iguanas, *Iguana iguana,* have long been a staple in the pet trade. As babies they are attractive, dinosaur-like little beasts, and as adults they are of even more impressive appearance. It is little wonder that they catch people's fancy. But where do they come from? And how do they get from there to the pet market?

In the 1960s and 1970s, all iguanas destined for the pet trade were collected from the wilds of their native lands. Today that is no longer true. Many, if not most, are being "farm-raised" in Latin America.

In the strictest sense, and to fully comply with the laws in some exporting countries, farm-raised means captive-bred and captive-hatched baby iguanas from captive-maintained breeding colonies. And in all fairness, this IS the actual origin of a great many of the baby iguanas now imported into the United States. Additionally, iguana "farmers" still catch and buy gravid female and newly hatched baby iguanas from the wild. Once the captured females lay their eggs, those eggs are incubated and hatched in captivity; the babies are mixed in with the rest of the hatchlings and all are exported.

Does this sort of harvest actually deplete wild populations of iguanas? Probably not. But the practice does provide fuel for more stringent future laws.

What happens once the babies have hatched? Newly hatched babies are nourished by egg yolk still retained in the body, and can be shipped as they hatch. As orders are received and sorted by the breeders, the young are gathered. They are packed (about fifty to a layer) into multitiered, burlap fronted and backed, wooden boxes. Exactly how many lizards go into each box depends on the size of both lizards and crates, and how many baby iguanas are available. At the beginning of the hatching-shipping season, thousands of the little lizards are exported weekly. Toward the end of mid-summer in the United States, this number may have dwindled to several hundred at which point the rate will hold steady for several months. To fill a special order, a few half-grown and adult iguanas may also be exported.

Babies or adults, all are transported by air. Airplane bin temperatures at 30,000 feet are more or less controlled, depending on the airline. But even the controlled temperatures are often far lower than ever experienced by a baby iguana in its homeland. Iguanas have no adaption process for low temperatures, and such temperatures, even for a short time, create stress.

Once received at the jobbers in the United States, the baby iguanas are released into "holding facilities." As often as not these are big, elongate, metal, livestock watering tanks with shavings in the bottom. Upward of a hundred baby iguanas are often held in each. Feeding, heating, and lighting in these facilities are often subminimal. Then comes the call from the wholesaler: "Send me 500 baby iguanas." And for the little lizards, the journey starts anew.

This time they are placed in a cloth bag containing crumpled newspapers.

At the wholesalers' baby green iguanas are bagged and placed in styrofoam boxes for shipment to pet stores.

The bags are placed in styrofoam shipping boxes, and again the iguanas are shipped northward (most jobbers are in southern California or Florida). Again, temperatures are suboptimal, the iguanas are additionally stressed, and they may be in their darkened shipping containers for two full days. But it's not over yet! The iguanas are shipped once more, from the whole-salers to the individual pet shops. More stress.

But finally the little lizards are at their destination and are (hopefully) being properly cared for by the folks at the shop.

The initial care given to these stressed baby lizards by the pet shop employees is very critical to the future well-being of the reptiles. They need warm temperatures, rehydra-tion, vitamins and minerals, and ample feedings of nutritious food right away. Denied any of these by the shop, the condition of the lizards will continue to deteriorate and may quickly become irreversible.

Then comes the final consumer—the (potential) hobbyist, past, present, or future—who often looks with open-eyed wonder at the iguanas and who often becomes infatuated with their prehistoric appearance. Generally speaking, if left to his or her own devices, the hobbyist will emerge from the shop with no iguana in tow. But, if that same adult is accompanied by an eight- or nine-year-old child, the saga is apt to end differently.

And it is for you that this pet own-er's manual is intended. Within these pages you will find the answers to most if not all of your questions, including what to be looking for when you choose your iguana.

The Two Green Iguanas

Throughout much of tropical Latin America and on a few of the islands of the Lesser Antilles dwell two species of the big, green lizards known popularly as green iguanas. Although of rather similar appearance, the two species are easily separated from one another by appearance and origin.

The more widely distributed of the two species, the common or green iguana, is *Iguana iguana*. It is found in Latin America and occurs naturally on some of the Lesser Antilles islands. It has been successfully introduced in recent times onto other Antillean islands, Hawaii, and into extreme southern Florida. All these areas boast a subtropical or tropical climate, heavy rainfall, and lush foliage.

Iguana iguana has several very distinctive identifying characteristics. Below the tympanum (external eardrum) are from one to several grossly enlarged, rounded scales. Many green iguanas from Mexico and northern Central America bear pronounced hornlike nubbins on the snout. At one time, these lizards were classified as a separate subspecies, *I. i. rhinolopha*, but this designation has been declared invalid and those former members of the subspecies are lumped in with the common green iguanas.

I. delicatissima, the "other" green iguana, is properly called the Antillean iguana. It is rarely, if ever, offered in the pet trade, and the only specimens I know of in the United States are in the Memphis zoo. The Antillean iguanas lack the grossly enlarged jowl scales, and are found only on certain of the Lesser Antilles islands. Some populations of the Antillean iguana seem to be diminishing, especially on the islands where the green iguana is also found. Where the two share a range, the green iguana seems the dominant species.

Physical Characteristics of the Common Green Iguana

The common green iguana is a bright green lizard that hatches out at 7 inches (17.8 cm) and ends up at more than 6 feet (1.8 m). As a hatchling and a young adult iguana, it bears a series of vertical dark bars on its body near the axis of the legs. More than two thirds of the total length is

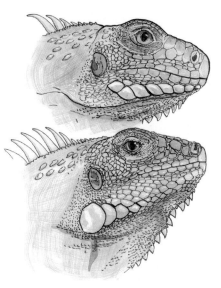

The large scales below the eardrum identify the green iguana (bottom). The Antillean green iguana (top) lacks these scales.

The tall crest, heavy jowls and large dewlap indicate this to be a typical adult male green iguana.

tail, which is used as a weapon against foes, i.e., any carnivore bigger than it is. An iguana of 3.5 to 4 feet (1–1.2 m) can raise welts with its tail; one demonstration will be enough to convince you.

Femoral Pores

Along the underside of the hind legs, iguanas have a series of pores called femoral pores. Best developed in the males, these pores secrete a waxy gray substance. The exudate from the femoral pores contains scenting molecules called pheromones, which are used to mark territory.

The Crest

Both males and females have vertebral crests, a row of enlarged, pointed scales along the spine, beginning at the head and decreasing in size down to the tail. The crest is larger and more pronounced in the males, and makes them look larger to their opponents. (Other iguanids that lack the crest, such as chuckwallas, inflate themselves with air to increase their size.)

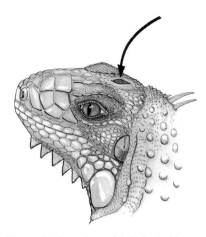

The parietal eye (arrow) is indicated by a modified scale.

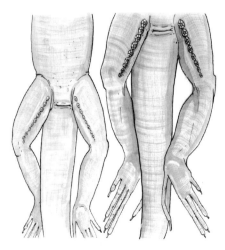

The femoral pores of the male iguana (right) are proportionately larger than those of the female (left).

The Dewlap

All iguanas bear a dewlap, a fold of skin under the throat that is displayed in courtship and territorial behaviors. Generally speaking, the males do most of the territorial displays, but the females also display. In adulthood, the males are larger, have heavier jowls, swollen temporal areas, and are brighter in overall coloration than females.

The Parietal Eye

Between and posterior to the eyes is a small grayish organ that looks like a modified scale. This is the parietal eye, which is sensitive to light and dark cycles (photoperiod) and so aids in the timing of the breeding cycle. The parietal eye on the lizard-like tuataras of New Zealand (which are so different from other lizards that they have their own separate family) is more advanced. In all lizards the parietal eye bears a lens and a retina, and is connected to the pineal body in the brain by a nerve.

10

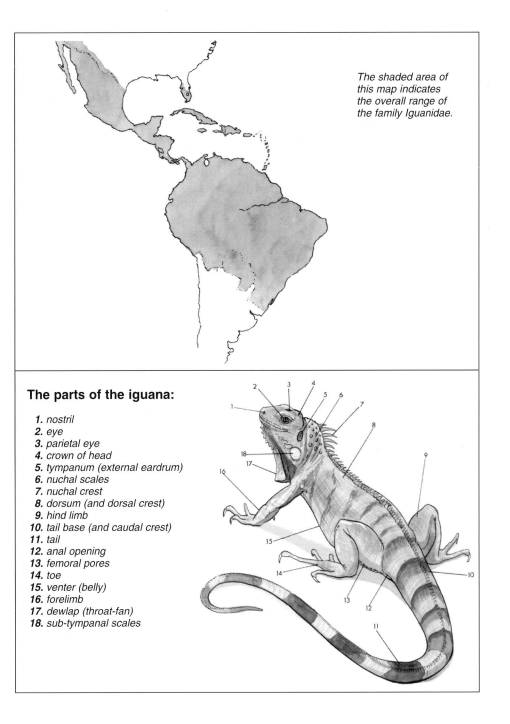

The shaded area of this map indicates the overall range of the family Iguanidae.

The parts of the iguana:

1. *nostril*
2. *eye*
3. *parietal eye*
4. *crown of head*
5. *tympanum (external eardrum)*
6. *nuchal scales*
7. *nuchal crest*
8. *dorsum (and dorsal crest)*
9. *hind limb*
10. *tail base (and caudal crest)*
11. *tail*
12. *anal opening*
13. *femoral pores*
14. *toe*
15. *venter (belly)*
16. *forelimb*
17. *dewlap (throat-fan)*
18. *sub-tympanal scales*

So You Want to Own an Iguana!

An in-depth look at the green iguana of the pet trade may reveal what often transpires when these lizards are first encountered.

"Mom, *Mom!* Look! Look Mom! Look at this lizard! What is it, Mom?"

The answer, usually tendered with considerably less enthusiasm than the query, informs: "It's an iguana, Butch."

"What's an iguana, Mom? Look, Mom! It's eating lettuce. Can I have one, Mom?"

Now, with any prior enthusiasm altogether lacking, comes Mom's response:

"*No!* Absolutely *not*! What would you want one of *those* things for?"

Good question, Mom. Why indeed? And yet when Mom and Butch leave the pet shop a baby green iguana goes with them.

The Question of Survival

But what are the chances of this lizard surviving? How do you choose a healthy iguana? Once chosen, how do you care for it? From where did it originally come and how did it get here? How big does it get? Will it *really* survive on lettuce?

Unfortunately, the chances of most baby iguanas surviving for extended periods in captivity are not at all good. Despite the fact that they are virtually always available in the pet trade, green iguanas have very specific care requirements. Furthermore, once an iguana's health has deteriorated to a

Look for a baby iguana with intense green coloration.

point where its illness is observable, it is quite difficult to reverse the downhill slide that ultimately results in the death of the lizard. With this latter fact in mind, it then becomes obvious that you *must* keep your iguana in tip-top condition at all times.

Choosing a Pet Store

Purchase your iguana from a *reputable* and *knowledgeable* source. Unfortunately, many pet shop employees know precious little about reptilian husbandry. This is most easily reflected by the conditions in which they keep their lizards. Look at the caging. Is it clean? Is there a light above one corner of the cage to provide a "hot spot?" Is the drinking water fresh? Is there food in the cage, and what sort of food? Iceberg lettuce has about the same nutritional value for iguanas as newsprint. They need dark greens such as romaine, collard, mustard, and turnip greens, mixed with brightly colored vegetables and some fruits like tomatoes and cantaloupe.

Find a pet shop with employees who can accurately answer your questions. To determine accuracy, compare some of their answers to your questions to the information contained in this book or in your other readings. They should jibe. If the pet shop employees cannot satisfactorily answer your questions, the chances are excellent that they are not caring for their iguanas properly. Shop elsewhere.

Choosing a Veterinarian

Find a veterinarian who is well versed in reptile husbandry. You will quite likely need him or her sooner or later (and unfortunately it will more often than not be sooner than later). The treatment of reptiles is a specialty practice. Not all veterinarians will be able to adequately diagnose and treat an ailing iguana. Ask your pet shop to recommend a veterinarian, or spend some time with a phone and a telephone directory and call veterinarians in your area. You might as well ask what an office call will cost, so you'll know ahead of time.

Considerations Before Acquisition

Prepare the caging for your iguana. The chances are excellent that you will be purchasing a (somewhat) stressed lizard. It must have a secure cage in which it can feel safe, with lighting and food in place (see pages 17–27).

The purchase of an iguana should not be done on impulse. You must also understand that iguanas have very specific needs for their survival. If you buy or are given an iguana, you are obligated to provide it with the habitat and food it needs. The entire procedure, from purchase to health care to feeding to caging, needs to be thought through. Properly kept, a green iguana will be 2 feet (0.6 m) long at the end of the first year, and 3 feet (0.9 m) long at the end of the second year. Its caging requirements will grow proportionately. Are you ready to share your quarters with a 5- or 6-foot (1.5–1.8 m) long lizard? Of course, an iguana will not run up your phone bill or hide the remote to your TV. It will, however, require a changing and specialized diet, and a sizable area to roam.

Choosing a Healthy Iguana

How do you choose a healthy iguana? You let the iguana help you to do so. There are several criteria that you must consider. The initial health of your lizard may determine *all else* about its captive life.

Skin Color

Both the intensity of color and the very color itself, can aid you in choosing a healthy baby iguana. Baby green iguanas are green (rarely blue-green and even more rarely a grayish

When buying, choose an alert, bright-eyed baby with good coloration.

girdle) starkly evident. As the health of an iguana deteriorates, the lizard will appear ever more bony and emaciated.

Demeanor

Choose a baby iguana that is alert and that has bright eyes that watch the movements around it—your movements, for example. And if among those alert, bright-eyed babies, there is one that is calm (or at least relatively so) choose it. The more nervous a baby iguana is, the harder it will be to tame it!

If you can, watch the iguanas as food is placed in the cage. You want an iguana that approaches the food and begins chowing down. Admittedly, you may be in the pet shop after the iguanas have eaten their fill and are no longer interested in the food. But for obvious reasons, you want an iguana that recognizes food as something to be eaten.

Captive-bred vs. Wild-caught Iguanas

Generally speaking, support domestic herpetological efforts if at all possible. Buy iguanas that have been captive-bred and captive-hatched. Not only will this be an ecologically wise decision on your part, but there's a very practical reason as well. Your lizard will be healthier. A domestically bred and hatched lizard will be relatively parasite-free or have a minimum parasite load. Because food insects carry parasites, and iguanas eat insects, the completely parasite-free iguana may not exist. Captive-produced iguanas are usually less stressed than wild-caught specimens, and the balance between host and parasite is less apt to become altered.

My tip: For a very short period of time during the year, newly hatched baby iguanas are available to the pet trade. These may be either captive-hatched or imported. These are tiny

green), not a sickly, pasty green, but vibrant and intense—the color of the healthy leaves of a new growing plant. (It is the bright green color that draws most people to a display of baby iguanas, and interestingly enough, this same color permits the babies to blend imperceptibly with the foliage in their home country.) Unless the baby iguana is preparing to shed its skin (something that it does periodically throughout its life), a dull green color indicates poor health; a yellow-green often indicates impending death. However, vertical dark markings that may vary both in number and intensity are usually present. The markings near the shoulder and the hips are usually the most prominent.

Body Weight

Choose an iguana that has good body weight. Do not purchase one that has the bones (especially the pelvic

Checklist for Healthy Iguanas

	Good Signs	Warning Signs
Size	newly hatched babies, 7 to 12 inches (7.8–30.5 cm) long are best	larger iguanas hard to tame or handle; may not feed
Color	look for bright green coloration	yellowish color; mottled gray-green
Demeanor	alert and interested in surroundings but not frightened	apathetic attitude; closed eyes; "sleeping"
Behavior	facing the front of the terrarium	avoiding front; hiding in corner
	actively sunning under heat lamp	uninterested or too weak to move to heat lamp
Appearance	no visible wounds or damage; no broken tail or limbs; no banged up nose	wounds incurred in shipment will be slow to heal in a stressed lizard
Feeding	runs to food dish when it is placed in terrarium; begins to feed readily	no interest in food

animals, perhaps 7 or 8 inches (17.8–20.3 cm) in overall length, and still heavy with the egg yolk that sustained them through a prolonged incubation. Most have not yet fed, hence have not yet been weakened by parasites. Should you be considering an iguana for a pet, these are, by far, the very best candidates!

And Bear in Mind...

Never (not even for humanitarian reasons) choose an iguana with dull, sunken eyes and listless mien. It will probably not survive. Always choose an iguana from a clean cage that has been provided with ample fresh drinking water, a warmed and well-illuminated basking area, *and* full-spectrum lighting (see page 21). The importance of this latter item, although still being researched, seems significant in inducing "natural" or "normal" behavior.

As green iguanas grow, they lose the intensity of color that typifies the healthy young. Adults over 3 feet (0.9 m) are predominantly grayish green. They retain the dark markings of the juveniles. Occasional adults may be brick red (these are remarkably beautiful animals and consequently are much in demand by hobbyists).

Sadly, most subadult and adult iguanas are even more difficult to acclimate than the hatchlings. They are also correspondingly more difficult to handle. Take particular care in choosing one. As with a baby or juvenile, the eyes of

Chris McQuade demonstrates how to hold a frisky adult iguana.

an adult should be neither sunken nor dull and listless, nor should the lizard appear thin and emaciated.

Remember that wild adults can bite and scratch savagely and slap resoundingly with their tails. They have gotten to be adults by fighting anything that looks like an enemy, and you look pretty suspicious to them. Be sure you are able to handle and care for a large iguana before the purchase. Most wild-caught, imported iguanas will be very difficult to tame, and hence are dismal pet candidates. They are also invariably heavily parasitized.

Caging Your Green Iguana

Caging and Iguana Behavior

In the wild, individual iguanas wander over a large area. They climb agilely, swim adeptly, and spend considerable time on the ground as well. They move quickly from one area to another with no barricades. Theirs is truly a three-dimensional existence.

Although it would be a virtual impossibility to offer such varied and spacious quarters to a captive iguana, large caging containing strategically placed "cage furniture," having a controlled, tropical temperature, and being illuminated by full-spectrum lighting is fairly easy to achieve. Proper caging is vital to your lizard's well-being.

You may wonder how an iguana can possibly get enough exercise within its cage. It would be difficult to build a cage that large. There are options, however. Once your iguana is acclimated to you and to its cage, you may want to give it more room. If you have a room in which your iguana can safely wander, you could open the cage but retain the cage's "hot spot" for warming and the food and water dishes. Your iguana can then roam at will, returning to its cage for food and water, and for basking. The disadvantage is that this will decrease the tameness of your lizard; it is the forced socialization with its owner that keeps the lizard tame.

Although baby and subadult iguanas can be housed communally, adults are solitary lizards that stake out their territories and defend those territories vigorously against incursions by other iguanas. The culminating interactions between two wild males can be particularly savage; those against females are usually less so. This is especially so if the female happens to be sexually receptive.

Two maturing male iguanas that have been housed together since babyhood are very likely to become incompatible with age. Occasionally a male and a female will prove less antagonistic. If you decide you'd like more than one iguana, you need to be ready to provide separate housing.

Enclosure Size

Enclosure size will, of course, depend on how big your iguana is and whether or not it is taken out for exercise or otherwise regularly handled.

For one or two hatchling, or very young iguanas, a standard 29- or 30-gallon (109.8–113.6 L) aquarium will suffice. For one or two 18 to 30 inchers (45.7–76.2 cm), a 50-gallon (189.3 L) aquarium will provide satisfactory space.

Your cage top should be tight fitting and secured in a manner to prevent your iguana from pushing it upward and escaping. Even tame, relatively content iguanas will occasionally attempt escape. Commercially made terrarium tops that clamp tightly into place are now available in most pet shops. If you choose to make your own wood-framed case, it is a small matter to hinge and secure a top. If the top is separate from the cage, use clamps or place a brick atop each end to discourage unauthorized "wanderings." This may not be attractive, but it is functional.

You want to opt for wood and wire or plastic and wire tops. This allows air circulation and permits ultraviolet (UV) rays from the full-spectrum bulbs to pass through and reach your lizards.

As your iguana grows, it will require correspondingly more space, and the more space the cage will take in your home. A 3-foot (0.9 m) long iguana will graduate to a custom-built cage that will quickly become the focal point of a room, if only by the space it requires.

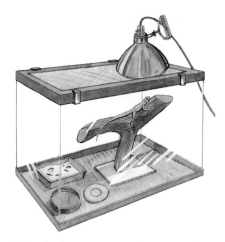

This simple arrangement is adequate for a baby iguana.

outside of the framework. The bottom can be a piece of plywood—0.75 inch (19 mm) is best, but 0.5 inch (12.7 mm) will do—or can be wire mesh if the cage sits atop a bed of newspaper. During the colder months, you may have to staple plastic to the outside to facilitate warming the cage. The supporting braces will need to be at least 2 × 2s or better, 2 × 4s, and the wire

Once tame, your iguana may spend his time sitting quietly on your shoulder.

Don't let the term "custom-made" scare you. Anyone with even a very moderate skill in carpentry can make a very suitable cage in an evening's time. If you know how to hammer, staple, and use a saw, you can make a cage. (Despite the fact that I am not a skilled carpenter, I built the moveable cages shown in the photographs in a half day.)

A simple cage begins with a wooden framework. Wire mesh is stapled to the

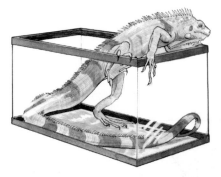

This is a clear case of too little cage for too much iguana.

mesh 1 × .5 inch (25 × 12.5 mm). A smaller mesh is apt to catch the iguana's toenails and injure the toes. The mesh must be welded to prevent the lizard from abrading its nose if it tries to escape. The braces can be nailed or screwed together and the mesh stapled on with a heavy duty staple gun. Be sure the door is large enough for you to reach to the bottom of the cage, to clean it, or add another door at the bottom of the cage for this purpose.

If you prefer a heavier cage, you can build one from plywood sheeting with wood-framed glass doors. The plywood cage will require sizable screened ventilation panels on each end. If wire is used in the ventilation panels, make certain it is welded and a large enough mesh is used to avoid injury.

For a 4-foot (1.2 m) long adult iguana, a cage of 6-foot (1.8 m) length by approximately 30-inch (0.8 m) width by 6-foot (1.8 m) height (just narrow and low enough to be moved through a doorway) will be necessary. If your cage is of wood and wire construction, build casters (wheels) into its construction. If your cage is of glass construction, sit it on a plywood platform that is on casters. The bigger the casters, the better.

Keep big cages moveable. It will benefit you, and your lizard, in the long run. If your iguana is out of its cage roaming about your room or home much of the time, a cage of somewhat lesser dimensions would be acceptable. In all cases, your lizard should be able to stretch out its full length to bask.

OK. That took care of size. Now for the rest.

Lighting and Heat Sources

An iguana's lifestyle can be basically summed up in two words: "arboreal" and "heliothermic." These only sound complicated. Arboreal refers to trees, hence the climbing abilities of the iguanas. If there's a vertical

Caging of wood and wire construction may be made to fit an available niche.

A large cage can be easily made from wood and wire; casters make moving the cage easy.

When outside, sunlight will provide natural and beneficial light and warmth. Do not place a glass terrarium in the sun.

surface, iguanas want to climb it, whether the surface is drapes, your pants leg, or a branch.

Heliothermic relates to the sun and temperature. Iguanas regulate their body temperatures by basking in the sunlight, more often than not while stretched out on a limb of a tree. If they're warm, they can digest their food.

You will need to duplicate a sunlit habitat within the iguana's cage. Iguanas like to sprawl while basking. They will position themselves lengthwise along a sturdy limb, drooping their legs and part of their tails over the sides. In the wild, such basking stations are often above waterways into which the iguana may drop if startled. Although you won't be able to provide the waterway, you can provide the "sun"-warmed limb. A limb with bark will be much easier for your lizard to climb and cling to than a peeled one.

Although many of the smaller species of arboreal lizards do not hesitate to wander among the yielding twig tips, iguanas prefer the more substantial branches. Always provide your iguana with an elevated basking branch that is at least the diameter of its body, and preferably one and a half times body diameter. The limb(s) must be securely affixed, to prevent toppling. Your iguana will feel secure atop the limb.

Direct the warming beams of one (or if your iguana is large, two) floodlight bulb onto this perch from above. Be certain to position the bulb(s) so your iguana is unable to burn itself if it approaches the lamp. Currently I use large incandescent plant-growth bulbs for this purpose. However, a "full-spectrum" incandescent bulb has recently appeared on the market. This latter should not only provide warmth but some of the full-spectrum lighting that seems so necessary to the well-being of heliothermic lizards. A temperature of 95 to 98°F (35–36.7°C) (measured on the top of the basking limb) should be created. You'll need to provide this sort of lighting-and-hot spot for eight hours daily; like any other creatures, iguanas like it dark at night.

This type of light and warmth is mandatory for the long-term well-being of your iguana. It is at a body temperature of 89 to 95°F (31.7–35°C) that your lizard is the most disease resistant. I consider the "hot rocks" so often used with iguanas a very unnatural heat source for arboreal heliotherms. In nature, these lizards depend on alternating dark and light cycles to set their own body rhythms. They warm their bodies from the top down, by orienting and varying their body positions in relation to the warmth and position of the sun. Warming from the belly up is unnatural, and if your lizard happens to be gravid (pregnant), prolonged basking atop an overwarmed hot rock *may* cause egg damage. You might consider this a minor detail, but I feel it is an important consideration and a valid concern.

Should you opt to use a hot rock, you must be careful that the surface of the rock does not get hot enough to burn your lizard (remember it will be lying right atop the rock and its belly is less well protected than the back and side), and you must illuminate the surface of the rock besides. Remember, it is a combination of illumination *and* heat for which you are striving. Any heliothermic lizard—even one that is warmed—is distressed when brilliant illumination is not readily available.

Full-Spectrum Lighting

In all truthfulness, the jury is *still* out on the role of full-spectrum lighting. Many iguana keepers, and especially iguana breeders, consider the use of full-spectrum lighting mandatory. However, others have kept and bred iguanas (and other heliothermic lizard species) without ever using full-spectrum lighting. I am plagued with ambivalence on the subject. I have never considered *not* using full-spectrum lighting.

Certainly full-spectrum lighting cannot hurt your iguana. But does it really help? I feel that in an overall evaluation the answer to this would have to be yes.

Iguanas provided with full-spectrum lighting *seem* to display more normal behavior than those not so provided. And because normalcy is what you are striving for, I always suggest that full-spectrum fluorescent lighting be used in addition to the incandescent lighting already mentioned. To date the hands-down favorite among the fluorescent full-spectrum bulbs is that known as Vita-lite. It is the UV-A and UV-B rays that you are striving to provide your lizard with. Even when new, the

This is a simple, permanent outside cage for large iguanas.

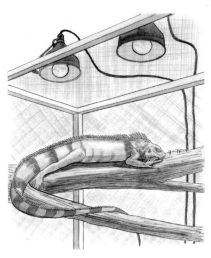

A basking iguana is a perfect picture of contentment.

"Full-spectrum" lighting is available in both fluorescent (with UV emissions) and incandescent (lacking UV emissions) bulbs. The latter might better be termed "color corrected."

amount of these rays emitted by a bulb is low. To gain any advantage from the bulb, your lizard must be able to bask within 6 to 12 inches (15.2–30.5 cm) of it. Typical of any fluorescent tube, Vita-lite bulbs give off little heat, so the lizard will not be burned even if he basks virtually against the bulb. Position the fixture accordingly.

When I first began to use Vita-lites in the 1970s, my lizards reacted immediately. They were more alert and less tolerant of handling. These changes were consistent for types as varied as iguanas, geckos, and blue tongues.

I truly believe that, over the long haul, your lizard will be better off for being provided with full-spectrum lighting. Full-spectrum bulbs are one way. But there's another, fairly easy way to provide this type of lighting, and it's as close as your back door.

Natural Sunlight

Natural, unfiltered sunlight unquestionably provides the best possible

lighting (and heat) for your iguana. Earlier I stressed that your cages always be able to pass through your doorways and be on casters. This will allow you to move your iguana—still securely caged—outdoors on warm, sunny days. In most cases the casters will allow a single person to accomplish this unwieldy task. Only cages constructed of wood and wire should be placed out in the sun. A glass terrarium filters out the UV. A glass terrarium, even with a screen top, will intensify and hold heat. This can literally cook your iguana in just a few minutes, even on a relatively cool day!

Be sure to provide a shaded area for your lizard even in the wood and wire cages.

The advantage to having a cage that is easily moved outside is to get the UV rays. Window glass and Plexiglas will filter out UV rays while allowing heat through. Remember, if your iguana is basking in a screened window, when temperature allows it, open the window. If the window is closed, the glass will filter out the UV rays.

What to Do If Your Iguana Escapes

It happens so easily. You forget to latch the cage after cleaning it; you've just taken out the water dish and the telephone rings; you've opened the cage and remembered that you turned on the microwave with nothing in it. Whatever the reason, when you get back to the cage, there's no iguana inside. Where do you look? Are there places that iguanas always hide?

To a certain degree, yes. Iguanas look for places where they will feel secure—high up (atop a curtain rod); where they are enclosed on three sides (atop books on a bookshelf); under things (the sofa, for example, especially if the bottom muslin covering is torn and it can crawl inside); or behind

Avoiding Electrical Accidents

It is important to use caution when handling electrical equipment and wiring, which are particularly hazardous when used in connection with water. Always observe the following safeguards carefully:

• Before using any of the electrical equipment described in this book, check to be sure that it carries the UL symbol.

• Keep all lamps away from water or spray.

• Before using any equipment in water, check the label to make sure it is suitable for underwater use.

• Disconnect the main electrical plug before you begin any work in a water terrarium or touch any equipment.

• Be sure that the electric current you use passes through a central fuse box or circuit-breaker system. Such a system should only be installed by a licensed electrician.

Even a trouser leg is an invitation to climb.

needs first aid, take care of the problem. Then return your pet to its cage, provide food and water—and make sure you latch the cage before you leave.

things (a dresser or a bookcase). Check in corners and places where two or more surfaces come together to provide a secretive nook. Look under the beds—especially if they are covered with bedspreads that reach to the floor, and check behind the draperies.

The good news is that iguanas tend to forget that to hide completely their tails also need to be out of sight. Look for a tell-tail, dangling from your curtains, hanging over the edge of a shelf, or extending out from behind the pots and pans in your cupboard.

When you do locate your pet, scoop it up (remember iguanas don't like to be grabbed from above) and check for damages. Your household has a variety of ways that an iguana can hurt itself—bruise from running into walls, burns acquired when it lodged itself behind a hot radiator, and so on. If your iguana

For an iguana loose in your house or apartment, every nook and cranny provides an invitation to hide.

A healthy, bright-eyed baby iguana sits in front of an adult.

Once acclimated, a baby iguana will feed readily and grow rapidly.

Adult iguanas are impressive lizards.

HOW-TO:
Furnishing and Cleaning the Cage

The use, size, and placement of basking limbs in the iguana enclosure have already been discussed. What more is necessary, to give the animal a feeling of security? Some keepers like to provide their iguana with a hiding box, additional limbs, and greenery.

Greenery

Because iguanas are largely herbivorous they will not hesitate to chomp down on the leaves of living plants. It is imperative, then, that if live plants are used they be of non-poisonous types. Wandering Jew might be a good choice, although you will have to resign yourself to replacing the plant as it is sampled. It is also important that if you use greenhouse plants no insecticides, neither contact nor systemic, nor spray-on fertilizers are present. The

Cardboard cartons can be used for hide boxes and when soiled, thrown away.

only fertilizer you can safely use is a concealed fertilizer, like the fertilizer sticks you insert into the soil.

Plastic plants make a lot of sense. They can be washed, as they become soiled. They are generally sturdy enough to bear up under an iguana's weight, and you can simply staple the foliage where you want it. Iguanas generally test the edibility of the plants with their tongue, then lose interest.

A Hide Box

Even a simple cardboard box with an entrance hole will provide security for your iguana. You may want to use a hide box only on a limited basis. If your iguana can conceal itself every time you approach it, it may never become tame. Whereas a hide box might be a good idea for a brand-new iguana, I would remove it after a period of two weeks or so.

The Flooring

The floor covering of your cage can consist of any number of items. Newspaper, wrapping paper, astroturf, indoor-outdoor carpeting, cypress or aspen shavings (never cedar; it can be toxic to your lizard), or even rabbit food (compressed alfalfa pellets) are all ideal. The papers, shavings, and rabbit food can be discarded when soiled; the carpets can be washed when dirty, then dried and replaced.

Many persons have found that their iguanas will repeatedly defecate in a particular area of their cage. Some iguanas defecate in their water

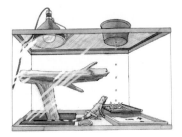

A drip-bucket may be necessary to induce a newly imported baby iguana to drink.

dishes (which must then be cleaned immediately), but others will quickly adopt a kitty litter pan containing a little sand. The cleaning of the pan is then a simple matter.

Fresh Water

A pan or tray of fresh drinking water should always be available to your iguana. Many iguanas enjoy soaking in tepid water as much as drinking it, and will spend considerable time in their water trays, size permitting.

Some iguanas do not like to drink from a pool of still water. Make a "drip bucket" by punching a small slit or hole with a pocketknife in the bottom of a quart-sized plastic bucket. Each morning, fill the bucket with water and place it atop the cage where it can drip through the top screening into the water dish below. (Make sure the water dish is big enough to hold the water from the drip bucket, or you'll end up with a wet cage.) Empty and clean the water dish daily.

Misting Techniques

Some iguanas enjoy an occasional misting with a fine spray of tepid water. When you use a mister to offer water to your iguana, don't aim at the animal. Water squirted directly at an iguana may be interpreted by the lizard as a threat, and your iguana could panic. Aim the mister upwards so the mist falls like rain onto the iguana and its surroundings. You'll find your iguana perks up as the droplets descend, and if thirsty, will bend to lap droplets from its log.

Cleaning the Cage

In the wild, iguanas can move around and the buildup of debris is not a problem. Unfinished leaves wither and fall to the ground and decay, and partially eaten fruit is eaten by other animals. In captivity, conditions change. As the owner, you'll need to clean your

A clean terrarium is a sanitary terrarium. Use a commercial or a home-made glass cleaner.

Misting is a suitable way to increase humidity and loosen shedding skin. Allow the mist to fall like raindrops rather than aiming it directly at the specimen.

iguana's cage at least twice weekly, both to avoid any possibility of harming your animal(s) through the contamination of the food or housing, and also for your own sake. If the substrate is mulch, you can clean less frequently than if you use substrates of carpeting, Astroturf, or newspaper. Here's a fast way to stay on top of cage cleaning.

Remove the iguanas and place them in another cage or in a clean trash can with a lid, so they can't jump out.

Pick up the moveable cage furniture and remove the flooring. If it's newspaper, throw it away. If the flooring is something more durable, such as Astroturf, shake it to remove debris. If the flooring is soiled, put it in your "to be washed" pile and find a fresh piece. If

you use mulch, be sure to change it at least once a month or when dirty.

If the enclosure is a glass terrarium, use a commercial glass cleaner to spray the cage, then wipe it out with paper towels. (You can make your own glass cleaner by putting a solution of 15 percent alcohol, 85 percent water, and two drops of dishwasher liquid in a spray bottle). If the enclosure is wooden or wire, brush out the debris and use window cleaner on stubborn spots.

Put fresh newspaper or new mulch down.

Replace the cage furniture. Wash the water bowl, refill it, and put it in place. Replace the food dish, making sure the food is fresh. Put your iguana(s) back into the cage, and replace the lid and heat lamp.

Understanding Iguanas

What to Expect from Your Iguana

If you expect a pet that is as affectionate as a dog, or even as responsive as a cat, then you're better off with a dog or a cat—*not* an iguana. Being a reptile, the responses of an iguana to various stimuli are entirely different than those of a domestic mammal or an easily tamable bird. As a matter of fact, some iguanas resist all overtures by their human keepers, never becoming tame. Many others will become reasonably tame, or at least not skittish, but steadfastly refuse to allow themselves to be picked up. Still others may allow some degree of petting but respond to a human touch on the head or nape by biting or lashing with their tail. And then there are the few, the very few, that become completely docile and allow their keepers nearly any degree of liberty they choose to take.

It is for one of these few that virtually all iguana keepers are hoping.

Behavior in the Wild

Keep in mind that, by nature, iguanas are rather solitary creatures. They only seek each other out during the breeding season, when the males fight each other for dominance and seek females for copulation. Territory- or cage-sharing between adult iguanas would be a very difficult adjustment and may not be possible. During your taming process, if you think of yourself as another, much larger iguana or as a possible predator, it may help you understand the viewpoint of *your* iguana.

The reason behind the male-male fighting during the breeding season is that the "winners"—the most dominant males—have the greatest success in breeding. To determine dominance, the lizards will begin by displaying. They will stand with their legs straight, inflate their bodies with air, fully distend the dewlap, then bite, lash with their tail, and exhale loudly in almost a hiss. In a real "knock down, drag-out" fight, the lizards may use their claws as well.

Females are less dominant, but may develop at least some territorial tendencies. Free-ranging female iguanas tend to be solitary creatures.

In the wild, any non-iguana-like creature approaching an iguana is quite apt to be a predator. Survival instinct dictates that the touched or grasped iguana either flee or fight. It is this instinct that you (and the iguana) must overcome.

Taming Your Iguana

So how do you overcome the flee or fight instinct? It may not be possible to do so, but you can at least try.

First, choose your iguana *very* carefully. Find one that is bright-eyed and alert but that does not whip with its tail when it is lifted. Choose a green iguana, which is just that— *brilliant* green. Do *not* accept one with a yellowish tinge to the color. An ill iguana or one that has been severely stressed will not welcome even the best intended overtures. Dark bars and/or spots (even very prominent ones) along the sides are OK. Many baby iguanas are so marked. Bear in mind that when frightened, as by capture, the color of an iguana fades somewhat. However, when the animal is left to its own devices, the brilliant green coloration should soon return.

Once your iguana is chosen and at home, try the following:

1. Until your iguana is completely used to its new home and to you, always move *very slowly!* An iguana will equate fast or sudden movements with danger more readily than it will slow movements. Try to pet your iguana with your hand, staying away from the nape area. Some enjoy having the throat area stroked. Repeat the action at least twice daily for two weeks.

2. You will soon learn what actions your iguana will readily tolerate and what actions it is more reluctant to allow. Concentrate on overcoming the negative responses. Again, always move *very slowly* when attempting to initiate trust.

Even a tame adult iguana can be a real handful, as shown by this 6-foot male held by Sheila Rodgers.

This is a pretty and healthy 4-foot long green iguana.

A male green iguana responding to a perceived threat.

3. If your iguana refuses to allow you to touch it or to be held in your hand, try the same exercise with a thin stick wrapped with cloth at the tip. Some iguanas initially find this a more acceptable alternative than touching by hand. If your iguana will allow this, shorten the stick a little every three or four days until it is at last discarded and your hand is touching your iguana.

4. Remember that most iguanas will resist being grasped from above. If you wish to lift your iguana, induce it to step onto your hand or arm. Once clinging securely, restrain the iguana (if necessary) with your other hand and lift all slowly. You will be able to move more quickly as your iguana becomes accustomed to this procedure.

5. When speaking to or in the same area as your iguana, use a calm, even tone of voice. You want your iguana to be relaxed as you approach it. Loud music or other noises may make your iguana nervous.

6. Iguana behavior changes after exposure to natural sunlight. The UV rays induce natural behavior, including aggression. If you have an outdoor enclosure for your iguana, or if you've wheeled its cage into the sunlight, expect your iguana to react quickly and unfavorably to any overtures you might make toward it. Other lizards, such as the Gila monster, exhibit the same sort of wildness upon exposure to natural sunlight. Don't take it personally; just bring the cage back indoors and let your iguana calm down for an hour or so before handling.

Tame iguanas of moderate size will ride comfortably on a crooked arm.

Let's Talk Diets

Dietary Considerations for the Green Iguana

The health of your iguana, as does the health of any other animal, begins with its diet. The importance of a good diet cannot be overemphasized. If given inadequate nutrition or the incorrect type of food, your iguana's health will ultimately decline. By the time the decline is tangible, it may be too late to reverse it.

Iguanas are not quick to show ill health. Often problems manifest themselves internally, your iguana all the while maintaining the bloom of health externally. It continues to eat, drink, bask, and otherwise respond "normally." Then one day you'll notice a swollen limb, or a slight yellowing to the previously bright green coloration, or a failure to respond as quickly as usual to the presence of food, and the "battle" to restore health to your pet lizard will truly be on.

The problem will be accentuated for, at times, a positive response by your iguana to a corrected regimen will seemingly be as slow as the decline.

Thus, formulating a proper diet at the beginning of your relationship with your iguana is mandatory. It should be of as broad a spectrum as possible and it *must* be done from the start. Whether or not the foods offered an iguana are good for it, your pet can and will become accustomed to consuming certain items. Like a child who will eat only hot dogs for lunch and supper, an iguana can develop bad eating habits. Once acclimated to such foods, many will resolutely resist change, and unlike children, the iguanas won't live long enough to outgrow the problems.

For young iguanas, or for ill iguanas, don't forget that the prepared baby foods (without added salt or sugar; those with added tapioca are fine) can be used as a starter food for those specimens reluctant to feed. There's a wide variety of pureed fruits and vegetables available. If the animal does not seem to recognize the food, use an eyedropper to place a very small amount well back in the mouth (pull gently on the dewlap to open). Be very careful not to place the food where it could be inhaled into the lungs; this can cause an irreversible mechanical pneumonia.

Strained vegetable baby foods can be used in an emergency for baby iguanas that are reluctant feeders.

A Reptilian Cow!

If the dietary propensities of an iguana were to be compared with those of a mammal, an apt comparison species would be a cow. As will that of its bovine equivalent, the bacterial content of an iguana's gut will quickly and effectively break down and digest the high-cellulose content of leaves and other plant parts.

To understand its dietary requirements, it is necessary to understand a few pertinent physiological facts about your iguana.

For a few days after hatching, your iguana is nourished by the egg yolk in its body. However, even within that few day period, a hatchling iguana will begin sampling foods.

This very tame iguana enjoys its food and eats readily, even when held.

Although even as a baby a green iguana is basically a leafeater, it may opportunistically sample beetles and other insects, a nestling bird, or a nestling mouse. Like a young animal of any species, it will literally taste everything it comes across. However, in the wild, the base diet of an iguana, whether juvenile or adult, will be the foliage and fruits that surround it. As they mature, green iguanas show less predilection to consume animal matter.

Coprophagy (the eating of feces) is not an abnormal behavior for iguanas. Oddly enough, this behavior has a practical side. This is how the young iguanas acquire the beneficial gut bacteria needed to break down the difficult-to-digest high-cellulose content of the foliage diet. (Unfortunately, coprophagy also means the young iguana will pick up endoparasites and other unwanted organisms as well.) Young iguanas that lack the gut bacteria will have trouble digesting their

food, as will an iguana that has had antibiotics administered orally; the antibiotics kill the beneficial bacteria as well as the pathogens. If your iguana is having problems digesting its food, the lack of gut bacteria may be part of the problem.

As your iguana grows, its dietary preferences and needs will change, and the diet you provide must reflect these changes.

Baby iguanas may or may not be quite omnivorous for the first few months of their lives. In the wild, many consume not only plant material, but may eat virtually every suitably-sized, non-noxious protein-laden insect species that they happen across at one time or another. Other baby iguanas may decline insects, opting instead for the carbohydrate diet of leaves and other vegetation that will comprise the later diets of all.

If given an opportunity, captives will show the same individuality. Whereas protein in the form of crickets, the larvae of tenebrionid beetles (mealworms and giant mealworms), grasshoppers, and even newly born mice will be eagerly devoured by some, others will disdain these offerings, instead preferring vegetation.

In the wild, with growth, even the iguana that as a baby readily accepts insects will begin to alter its diet. Of its own accord it will consume an ever greater proportion of vegetation, until its insect repast is limited to a very occasional snack.

You need to provide this type of latitude in captivity. It is necessary for you, the keeper, to provide your iguana with its preferred diet and the necessary changes. If your iguana has been one of those that have been eating a small proportion of insects as a baby, as it grows, begin decreasing the number of insects offered and

A variety of food is the spice of an iguana's life. Animal matter should be fed very sparingly, if at all.

Dietary Pyramid for Iguanas
for Calcium-Phosphorous Balance

Feed in decreasing proportions as you proceed up the pyramid

animal protein
baby mice
crickets
mealworms

apple	green beans	plums
avocado	honeydew melon	raspberries
blackberries	Hubbard squash	strawberries
blueberries	huckleberries	summer squash
cantaloupe	okra	tofu
carrots	peaches	
grapefruit	pears	
alfalfa	dandelion greens	leaf lettuce
beet greens	endive	mustard greens
Boston bibb	escarole	orange
broccoli stems and leaves	green cabbage	romaine lettuce
Chinese cabbage	kale	tangerine
collards	kohlrabi	turnip greens

increase the amount of vegetation. You may think this unfair, but it is necessary for the long-term health of your iguana. By the time it is a year old, your iguana should be getting insects or a suitably sized mouse only as a *very occasional* treat.

The nutritional value of the various plants and plant parts that are available to you differ greatly in food value. Not all of those that are of benefit in a human diet are similarly beneficial to your iguana. As a matter of fact, some plants considered safe for human consumption can actually be bad for your iguana. Other plants and plant parts, although not actually toxic, can react adversely with other components of your iguana's diet and cause harm over a period of time.

Raising Insects

Although green iguanas need a very limited amount of protein in the form of insects or mice, controlling the quality of the food you do offer is important. A poorly fed or otherwise unhealthy insect offers little but bulk when fed to your pet. Maintaining your insects in top-notch health should be a main concern of any herpetoculturist.

Before mentioning specific care for several of the more commonly used food insects, I feel that a mention of "gut-loading" is in order. In this technique your insects are fed an abundance of highly nutritious foods immediately before being offered as food to your iguanas. Calcium, vitamin D_3, fresh fruit and vegetables, fresh alfalfa and/or bean sprouts, honey, and vitamin and mineral-enhanced (chick) laying mash are only a few of the foods that may be considered for gut-loading insects. A commercially prepared gut-loading diet has only recently reached the pet marketplace. Insects quickly lose much of their food value if not continually fed an abundance of highly nourishing foodstuffs. Most insects eat rather continually, so it is much to the benefit of your lizards if you supply the insects with the highest possible quality diet.

All the food-insects offered to your iguana are commercially available. It may be your preference to avail yourself regularly of the various commercial sources. Certainly this is less time-consuming than breeding your own insects. However, by breeding your own you can assure that the highest possible diet is continually fed the insects. Even if procuring the insects commercially, you should begin feeding them the best diet possible as soon as you receive them.

Crickets: The gray cricket (*Acheta domesticus*) is now bred commercially by the millions both for fishing bait and for pet food. Other species are readily collected in small numbers beneath debris in fields, meadows, and open woodlands. If available in suitable sizes, all species of crickets are ideal as a protein source for your iguana.

Gray crickets are now so inexpensive that few hobbyists breed them themselves. If you need only a few, they can be purchased from local pet shops. If you keep insectivorous lizards in addition to iguanas, purchase your crickets from wholesale producers that advertise in fishing or reptile magazines. You will find the prices are quite reasonable when crickets are purchased in multiples of 1,000.

Feed your crickets a good and varied diet or one of the nutritious, specifically formulated cricket foods now on the market. Among other foods, fresh carrots, potatoes, broccoli, oranges, squash, sprouts, and chick laying mash will be readily consumed. All offered foods should be sprinkled with calcium and vitamin D_3, not for the crickets, but for the benefit of the iguanas to which the crickets are fed. Crickets can and will be cannibalistic if crowded or under-fed. Although crickets will get much of the moisture requirements from their fruit and vegetables, they will also appreciate a water source. Crickets will drown easily if they are given just a plain, shallow dish of water. Instead, place cotton balls, a sponge, or even pebbles or aquarium gravel in the water dish. These will give the crickets sufficient purchase to climb back out if they should happen to fall in.

Keep crumpled newspapers, the center tubes from rolls of paper towels, or other such hiding areas in the crickets' cage. I prefer the paper towel tubes for they can be lifted and the requisite number of crickets shaken from inside them into the cage or a transportation jar. This makes handling the fast moving, agile insects easy. A tightly covered 20-gallon (75.7 L) long tank will temporarily house 1,000 crickets. A substrate of sawdust, soil, vermiculite, or other such medium should be present. This must be changed often to prevent excessive odor from the insects.

If you choose to breed your own crickets, this is not difficult. Keep the cricket cage between 76 and 86°F (24.4–30°C). Place a shallow dish of slightly moistened sand, vermiculite, or even cotton balls on the floor of the cage. The material in this dish will be the laying medium and will need to be kept very slightly moistened throughout the laying, incubation, and hatching process. Adult crickets are easily sexed. Females will have three "tubes" (the central one being the egg-depositing ovipositor) projecting from the rear of their bodies. Males lack the central ovipositor. The ovipositor is inserted into the laying medium and the eggs expelled. The eggs will hatch in from eight to twenty days, the duration being determined by cricket species and tank temperature.

Nutritious food should always be available to the baby cricket.

My tip: Should you decide to raise crickets, expect some of them to get out. What happens? Not much, except your house will sound like mine, with crickets chirping all year round. I think it is a cheerful sound.

Grasshoppers and locusts (*Locusta* sp. and *Shistocerca* sp. in part): Although migratory and other locusts are not available in the United States, they are widely used as reptile foods in European and Asian countries. These can be bred or collected. Grasshoppers can be field collected in the United States by the deft wielding of a field net. However, grasshoppers are fast and may be difficult to collect.

In some southern areas large, slow grasshoppers called "lubbers" may be found. Many of these have a brightly colored (often black and yellow or red) nymphal stage that can be fatally toxic if eaten by your iguanas. The tan and buff adults seem to be less toxic but their use as a food item is contraindicated.

Waxworms (*Galleria* sp.): The "waxworm" is really a caterpillar, the larval stage of the wax moth that frequently infests neglected beehives. These are available commercially from many sources. Check the ads in any reptile and amphibian magazine for wholesale distributors. Some pet shops also carry waxworms. If you buy wholesale quantities of wax-worms, you will need to feed them. Chick laying mash, wheat germ, honey, and yeast mixed into a syrupy paste will serve adequately as the diet for these insects.

Giant mealworms (*Zoophobas* sp.): These are the larvae of a South American beetle. They are rather new in the herpetocultural trade and at present (1994), their ready availability is being threatened in the United States by the Department of

Agriculture. This is unfortunate, for *Zoophobas* have proven to be of great value to reptile breeders.

Zoophobas can be kept in quantity in shallow plastic trays containing an inch (2.5 cm) or so of sawdust.

Although they are still available in many areas of the United States and virtually all over Europe and Asia, it would seem prudent for American herpetoculturists to breed their own.

To do this, place one mealworm each in a series of empty film canisters or other similar small container (to induce pupation) that contains some sawdust, bran, or oats. After a few days the worm will pupate, eventually metamorphosing into a fair-sized black beetle. The beetles can be placed together in a plastic tub, containing a sawdust substrate and some old cracked limbs and twigs for egg laying (the female beetles deposit their eggs in the crack in the limbs). The beetles and their larvae can be fed vegetables, fruits, oat, and bran. The mealworms will obtain all of their moisture requirements from the fresh vegetables and fruit.

You can keep two colonies rotating to assure that you have all sizes of the larvae you will need to offer your iguanas. Although giant mealworms seem more easily digested by the lizards than common mealworms, neither species should be fed in excess. Once a week will be sufficient for your iguanas; if you keep any insectivorous lizards, they would welcome the "leftovers."

Mealworms (*Tenebrio molitor*): Long a favorite of neophyte reptile and amphibian keepers, mealworms should actually be fed sparingly. They are easily kept and bred in plastic receptacles containing bran (available at your local livestock feed store) for food and a potato or apple for their moisture requirements. It takes no special measures to breed these insects.

Roaches: Although these can be bred, it is nearly as easy to collect roaches as needed. Roaches, of one or more species, are present over much of the world. The size of the roach proffered must be tailored to the size of the iguana being fed. One or two small roaches a week will be plenty.

Termites: Collect fresh as necessary. Should you decide to hold "extras" over, they may be kept in some of the slightly dampened wood in which you originally found them. Termites are most easily collected during the damp weather of spring and summer. One particularly enterprising hobbyist has placed a huge pile of wood shavings some distance from his home, then introduced termites to the pile. From this he can collect these little insects nearly year-round. (I must mention, however, that this approach to breeding termites has proven detrimental to the structural integrity of his wood frame house!)

Caution: If you do decide to feed your iguana termites, it is definitely best to collect these insects as needed, then use them immediately.

Raising Mice

Mice are easily bred. A single male to two or three females in a 10-gallon (37.9 L) tank (or a rodent breeding cage) will produce a rather steady supply of babies that can be fed to your growing iguanas. *Do not* use cedar bedding for your mice. The phenols contained in cedar can be harmful to your iguana. Use aspen or pine shavings.

Feed your mice either a "lab-chow" diet that is specifically formulated for them or a healthy mixture of seeds and vegetables. Fresh water must be present at all times.

Calcium, Phosphorus, Vitamin D$_3$, and Ultraviolet Lighting

Four important components in the well-being of your iguana are calcium, phosphorus, vitamin D$_3$, and illumination in the ultraviolet spectrum. Iguanas need a lot of calcium. Approximately twice as much calcium as phosphorus should be present in the diet of your iguana. Vitamin D$_3$ aids in the absorption of the calcium.

Ultraviolet (UV) rays may be separated into two groups, UV-A and UV-B. UV-A induces normal activity patterns in reptiles, whereas UV-B apparently helps your lizards to synthesize vitamin D$_3$.

The UV spectrum of lighting may be supplied through the use of full-spectrum bulbs or natural sunlight (see Lighting and Heat Sources, page 21). I strongly recommend the latter whenever and wherever possible.

Houseplants, Ornamental Plants and Spinach

It is best to consider all house and ornamental plants as toxic unless otherwise instructed. Some of the "OK" types are listed below. The toxic varieties may vary in toxicity, but none should be offered as a food source. Even some commonly grown garden vegetables can, if offered over a period of time, seriously compromise the health of your iguana. The compounds in these plants can profoundly affect the ability of your iguana to properly metabolize calcium, or they may have other deleterious effects. Feeding your iguana these plants on a regular basis can do far more harm than good.

Spinach is one plant you want to avoid. Spinach has a high level of phosphorus and a fairly low level of calcium, and it also contains oxalic acid.

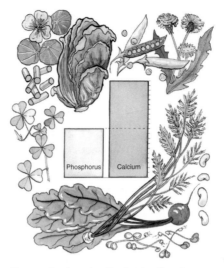

Frequently changing the foods offered your iguana will prevent both imprinting and boredom, but you must try to provide twice as much calcium as phosphorus. Caution! Do not mistake the harmful oxalis (wood sorrel) for beneficial clover.

The oxalic acid binds with the calcium present to form calcium oxalate, a compound detrimental to your iguana.

Besides preventing the proper metabolism of calcium, the calcium oxalate can cause kidney damage and ultimately, uremia. Components normally excreted in the urine will instead build up in the bloodstream, causing severe health problems and eventually, death. Save the spinach for yourself and avoid feeding it to your iguanas even on a casual basis.

Another plant to avoid is the pretty little wood sorrel (*Oxalis* sp.) This is a commonly grown house and garden plant as well as a naturally occurring wildflower. It also contains high levels of oxalic acid. Neither the clover-like leaves nor the flowers should be fed to your iguana.

There are a great many completely safe and very beneficial natural foods readily available. Speaking in generalities, vegetables are often more nutritious than fruits, and iguanas often consider the appropriate leafy vegetables the most natural of all. You may discover that some of your "shopping" can be done in your own backyard, at the local feed store, or at the corner fruit and vegetable stand. Some food plants can be raised on your porch or windowsill. Offer a wide variety of foods, not that you need to offer 12 different types of food at each feeding, but rather if you offer foods *a,b,c,* and *d* one week, offer *b,c,d,* and *e* the next, and *c,d,e* and *a* the following week.

When at all possible, check on the calcium and phosphorous content. You and your iguanas want a high-calcium:low-phosphorous ratio in the foodstuffs offered. Use this booklet as a guide, or obtain *Composition of Foods*, U.S. Department of Agriculture, Handbook Number 8, Washington DC for foods not listed here.

Dandelion leaves and flowers are excellent foods.

Alfalfa: hay or pelleted animal foods (packaged and sold for guinea pigs and rabbits). These animal foods are ground or shredded alfalfa or hay that is then compressed into green pellets about a 0.25-inch (6.4 mm) square. You buy them by the pound or by the package at feed stores or at pet stores. I have seen even small iguanas eat these pellets with no difficulty.

Berries: black, straw, mulberry, fruits, and leaves. Because of the high phosphorus to calcium ratio, the berries should be fed sparingly. Berries of any sort are not high in food value, but they certainly can add flavor and color to a diet.

Broccoli: Stems and leaves are excellent. Flowerets have high phosphorus to calcium ratio and should be fed sparingly if at all. You can buy the frozen variety and use the flowerets for yourself and chop the stems to feed to your iguana.

Cabbage (including napa): A good food source. Remove the thick stems and chop for the smaller iguanas.

Cauliflower (all parts): You can either buy this fresh, or buy the frozen bagged type and just thaw what is needed. Chop into small bite-sized pieces.

Cacti: The pads, flowers and fruit of such widely spread species as prickly pear are excellent foods. The spineless cultivars, commonly known as *Opuntia*, are the easier with which to work, but remember these still bear tiny, almost invisible colorless spines that imbed themselves in your hands where they will cause the most discomfort. Dice the cacti up into bite-sized pieces.

Clover: fresh or dried (if from lawns, be sure this is free of pesticide and spray-on fertilizer).

Grasses: fresh or dried (again, from lawns that are pesticide and fertilizer-free).

Greens: beet, carrot, collard, dandelion, mustard, and turnip. Where there are tough stems, either remove them or chop into bite-sized pieces.

Kale (limited amounts): Remove tough stems.

Legumes: beans, yellow, green, soy and other edible varieties (all plant parts), bean sprouts, and peas (including pods and leaves).

Lettuce: romaine, leaf, escarole.

Okra: Although this edible pod exudes a thick sap when diced, the pod is very nutritious and many iguanas like it.

Root crops: beets, rutabaga, and turnip leaves. Carrots, parsnips, and grated turnip roots have a high ratio of phosphorus to calcium, thus should be fed sparingly. Chop all into bite-sized pieces.

Soybean: There are several types of soybean foods to offer; this includes small cubes of tofu, the sprouts, or the green leaves.

Squash: acorn, yellow, zucchini, all parts including blossoms. The fruits should be finely grated. Pumpkin, a giant squash, is among the least beneficial of the commonly available forms.

Commonly available fruits such as nectarines and most melons have limited food value to iguanas. Apples, bananas, peaches, plums, and apricots are very high in phosphorus to calcium ratios, hence should be fed only sparingly and only when accompanied by foods with a higher calcium-phosphorus ratio, like romaine lettuce. Although watermelons have only a fair food value, they do have a more acceptable calcium to phosphorus ratio.

Some commonly grown garden plants and/or "weeds" that are safe foods and usually eagerly accepted by iguanas are nasturtiums, hibiscus, and dandelions. All parts of these plants are acceptable food items. Rose petals are also eagerly consumed.

Whole wheat bread, cut or torn into cubes or bite-sized pieces, is relished by many iguanas. If you have a bread-making machine, you may want to experiment with different grain combinations until you find one that both you and your iguana like.

Prepared Iguana Diets

An ever-increasing number of prepackaged iguana diets are making their appearance in the pet market. Most of those that are readily available, have been fully researched, and are rather complete in themselves. Some may be entirely so.

I believe that a variety of foods is best for your iguana. Although I would not hesitate to use the prepared diets as the main course, I would feel more confident if I augmented a prepared diet with fresh vegetables and an occasional fruit. The obvious advantages of a prepared diet are the ease of serving and the fact that the iguanas seem to like the diets.

Two examples of prepared iguana diets are Vite-A-Diet and Pretty Pets. You can buy these foods at your pet store or directly from the manufacturer (see page 85 for addresses).

Raising Your Own Food

If you choose to raise some of the food for your iguana, you can avoid pesticide contamination and also control the quality of the foodstuffs offered your lizard(s). Most vegetables can be container-raised with little trouble, once you understand the basic principles involved and have the patience to wait for your crop.

There are a couple of res You'll need to have en devote to the container to provide bright enough you cannot wheel your containers outside for insect pollination, you'll need to pollinate the blossoms yourself. Most importantly, you'll need to decide which crops will pay off with limited labor, time, and space.

There are a couple of shortcuts you can take. Check at your local grocery store or gardening supply store for plants that have already been started. You have seen seedling

Do not feed tomato leaves to your iguana.

Setting up your own "food factory" not only provides your iguana with fresh health foods, but provides greenery on your porch as well.

39

tomatoes, squash, and gardening plants such as hibiscus and leaf lettuce for sale; now you have a reason to buy these tiny plants.

Caution: Tomato leaves are toxic; carefully remove them before offering the fruit to your pet.

Perhaps the easiest to use containers are the decorative wooden "buckets" commonly used for porch gardening. You can fill these containers with potting soil and plant your seeds or seedlings. If you're starting with seeds, you might find it easier to get the seeds started in smaller flowerpots, then transfer them to the larger containers when they're about 4 inches (10.2 cm) high. The bucket containers work well with the larger plants like tomatoes or squash, although you'll need to add a stake and tie up the plant as it grows.

Don't forget that the plants will need light, and plenty of it. When the flowers appear, you'll need to put your plant where it can be pollinated by insects, or you'll need to place pollen from the pistils onto the stamen. Expect to wait three to four weeks for fruit to develop after fertilization.

Root crops such as carrots and parsnips yield both an edible root or tuber and edible leaves. The leaves are available as the plant sprouts; for the tubers, you'll need more time, up to 90 or 110 days.

Leafy vegetables will produce a usable crop faster than squash or tomatoes, simply because the leaves themselves are the crop. Once the romaine, escarole, or Boston Bibb lettuce is 2 inches (5 cm) high, you can begin to harvest the outside leaves. As the plant grows, you can continue to clip, and feed, the leaves. Clover will also respond to container growing, and the entire plant can be pulled and offered to your iguana.

Sprouts are another easily grown food. No matter which you choose—

Bean sprouts can be easily grown in jars in your kitchen.

mung bean or alfalfa—within a week you can offer fresh food to your lizards. Rather than a pot with soil, you'll need the seeds (purchased in bags from your grocery or health food store), water, and a series of quart jars that can stand on a countertop. Place ¼ cup of seeds in the jar, add enough water to cover them, and swish them around to rinse them. Empty the liquid and replace it with fresh water. Replace the top and let the jars sit for eight hours. If the jars rest on the side, the seeds will have more space and water around them.

At the end of eight hours, change the water. Swish the seeds around, empty the water, add new water, and rinse. Empty that water and add new water and cap the container. You'll notice that the water you're dumping from the first rinse has a distinct odor. That's why you're rinsing and dumping; you're disposing of the metabolic by-products of plant growth.

You'll need to repeat the rinse process three times a day: once when you wake up, another about 6 P.M., and again before you go to bed. You don't need to worry about fertilization or anything that complicated; you can just feed the sprouts to your lizards after four or five days. If you start a new jar every three days or so as you begin to empty out another, you'll always have fresh sprouts for your lizards (and for your vegetarian friends).

Vitamin and Mineral Supplements

Even with a well-rounded diet, it is unquestionably best to occasionally enhance your iguana's diet with vitamin and mineral supplements. Those supplements most recommended supply calcium at a ratio of at least 2:1 over phosphorus. Vitamin D_3 is also an important additive.

Whether or not vitamin A plays a detrimental role in reptile diets is open to conjecture at present. Because most fruits and vegetables are high in carotene, which is transformed into vitamin A, additional amounts in the form of additives seem superfluous.

Vitamin D_3 is *very* necessary to reptiles and amphibians. D_3 aids in the metabolizing of calcium. Whereas D_3 can be synthesized in adequate amounts from an average diet if your iguanas have access to natural sunlight, lesser amounts of UV-B will necessitate the addition of supplemental D_3. This holds true even with the much lauded full spectrum lighting. Although providing full-spectrum illumination is definitely better than not, the rays emitted by bulbs that are presently available are weak at best. Efficacy is lessened with bulb age. For your iguana to get any benefit from the bulbs, they must be both new and positioned very close to the lizard.

Supplemental calcium is always recommended. Exactly how much is necessary remains speculative. Rapidly growing baby and immature iguanas most certainly have a higher calcium requirement than adults do. Also, specimens recovering from rickets or metabolic bone disease will need more calcium than healthy ones.

Because ample phosphorus is almost always present in the normal diet of an iguana, many experienced and successful iguana keepers and breeders recommend the augmentation of the calcium alone. At my facility I have used both additives that supply only calcium and vitamin D_3 and additives containing a broader spectrum of ingredients. I can fault neither nor recommend one more strongly than the other. There are several excellent and commercially available calcium additives available both at your pet store and from your veterinarian.

The vitamin and mineral supplements that I have used over the years are:

Osteo-Form (calcium and phosphorus with vitamins). This is a product of Vet-A-Mix, Inc. of Shenandoah, Iowa. It contains an excellent ratio of calcium to phosphorus, about twice as much of the former as the latter. In addition, it contains a high amount of vitamin A and lesser amounts of vitamin D_3 and vitamin C.

Although this product contains more vitamin A than many herpetoculturists prefer, I have been very happy with the results produced by Osteo-Form. Osteo-Form is usually available from veterinarians and feed stores and in some pet shops.

Rep-Cal is 100 percent calcium and entirely devoid of phosphorus. It is a product of Rep-Cal Research Labs of Los Gatos, California. It also contains vitamin D_3.

How much should you offer and how frequently? For adult iguanas, meaning those longer than 3 feet (0.9 m), add a pinch of the powder over their food twice weekly. For younger, smaller iguanas in rapid growth (and they should be growing rapidly when they're young) add a small pinch of the powdered vitamin daily.

My tip: Iguanas with *unlimited* access to *natural, unfiltered* sunlight will require a lesser amount of vitamin and mineral additives than those having less or no access.

There are many brands of vitamin mineral supplements from which to choose. Keep the calcium to phosphorus ratio 2:1 or 3:1, with the calcium content being the higher.

Your Iguana's Health

Diet-related Health Problems

There are several diet-related health problems that can be alleviated or avoided entirely by the correct diet. Think of these as the sort of problems (rickets, scurvy) humans used to have before the benefits of vitamins were known.

Four broad types of diet-related health problems that may befall your pet iguana are metabolic bone disease (including rickets and demineralization), gout, vitamin and mineral imbalance, and elimination problems (constipation and diarrhea).

This chapter is by no means intended to be a complete coverage of all diet-related ills. Nor is it intended to supplant the diagnoses and treatments

Swollen limbs generally indicate metabolic bone disease, a problem which requires veterinary care.

offered by your qualified reptile veterinarian. A *qualified* reptile veterinarian can be your best friend during times of trouble. His or her recommendations should be followed to the letter.

Metabolic Bone Disease (MBD)
What, exactly, is metabolic bone disease (MBD)?

In simplified terms, MBD is the utilization of bone calcium deposits by the lizard to sustain life, due to improper diet or other causes.

The animal is not active and appears thin, except for its limbs. They seem plump. Sometimes the jawbones become shortened and the face looks chubby. That "plumpness" is your cue. It signifies a major health problem, one where the calcium is leached from the bones and bony tissue is replaced by a fibrous tissue. Your animal needs immediate veterinary care.

The technical names for metabolic bone disease are "nutritional secondary hyperthyroidism" and "fibrous osteodystrophy." Common names for the problem include rickets and demineralization. It is most commonly seen in iguanas and other lizards that have been fed a diet heavy in phosphorus and light in calcium, such as head lettuce, grapes, mealworms, spinach, and bananas. At first glance, this diet looks good, but when you check the phosphorus to calcium (P:Ca) levels, the diet is an iguana's worst nightmare come true.

To exist, an iguana needs a certain level of blood calcium. When the level of blood calcium drops below a certain percentage, the parathyroid glands then begin the complex process of drawing calcium from the bones to the blood. As the bones lose their rigidity, parts become overlaid with a fibrous tissue and deformities occur.

The preventative agent for MBD is calcium. The calcium/phosphorus balance of both dietary items and additives need be monitored carefully. The ratio of calcium should be maintained at no less than 2:1 over phosphorus.

Sufficient vitamin D_3 to enable your iguana to absorb and metabolize its calcium is also mandatory. Vitamin D_3 intake needs to be supplemented when your specimen does not have weekly access to direct, unfiltered sunlight. (The natural sunlight induces normal vitamin D_3 synthesis from digested foods, which, in turn, promotes calcium metabolism.)

Iguanas with unlimited access to natural, unfiltered (and I stress the word "unfiltered") sunlight require a lesser amount of vitamin D_3 and calcium additive than iguanas with little or no such access. Full-spectrum bulbs, although beneficial, produce only *small* amounts of the UV-A and UV-B rays so necessary to the synthesis and metabolizing of vitamins and minerals by your iguana. Regular vitamin and mineral augmentation of the diet of iguanas artificially illuminated is mandatory.

Even with a diet high in calcium, if the phosphorus ratio is elevated or vitamin D_3 is not present, MBD can and will occur. And, as I mentioned earlier, the debilitation is a long process through which your lizard will often continue eating and reacting "normally" until it is no longer able to do so.

MBD is treated by the injections of a synthetic hormone, calcium, and vitamin D. This new procedure was developed by Dr. Douglas Mader, a West Coast veterinarian. The treatment will work for MBD in its early stages, and in some (*but not all*) late stage cases.

Treatment for Your Ill Reptile

All too often an ailing animal is treated as a disposable commodity. This is especially true when reptiles are concerned. An oft heard comment is "I can buy a new one for less than the price of treatment."

It is no less expensive for veterinarians to treat a sick reptile than it is for them to treat an ailing mammal or bird. Because many of the treatments for reptiles require specific training on the part of the veterinarian, inexpensive diagnoses and medications should not be expected. Neither, do I believe, can a dollar value be placed on the life of your pet.

Always keep in mind that it is not the fault of the reptile that it is either in captivity or ill; both of those factors are due to wanting an exotic pet and lack of knowledge about what is necessary to successfully maintain such a pet.

Be prepared and willing to select and pay for trained professional help when it is necessary.

The treatment begins with lab work to determine the actual blood calcium levels. Once the diagnosis of MBD is confirmed, your veterinarian will begin three days of treatment with injectable calcium and (often) vitamin D. Oral calcium may also be administered. Following this period of vitamin and mineral stabilization, the synthetic hormone calcitonin-salmon is administered. This polypeptide hormone immediately begins to reverse bone resorption and to actually hasten the rebuilding of the bone structure. Because the levels of calcium and vitamin D have been boosted beyond normal day-to-day metabolic levels, the synthetic hormone can immediately utilize them in the restoration process.

With this treatment, veterinarians will be able to save the lives of many (but not all) animals with MBD.

But with care given to the diet of your lizard, MBD does not have to occur.

Gout

If insufficiently hydrated, an iguana may develop gout. Herbivorous reptiles are especially susceptible to this painful condition if foods too high in phosphorus are offered and if adequate, clean drinking water is not continually present. Iguanas are not extremely bright. Your iguana may not recognize its drinking water. The dish should be large enough for your lizard to soak in, and you may need to actually place the lizard into the water (of course, the cage "hot spot" will be warm enough to dry and warm the lizard when it leaves the water dish). Use the "drip bucket" method (see page 26) to create motion in the water's surface. Offer some water with an eyedropper. Spray the plastic plants in the cage with water, so your lizard can drink the droplets.

Proper hydration and a diet with the proper calcium-phosphorous balance almost ensures proper elimination of the causative urates.

Vitamin and Mineral Imbalances

Throughout the text, the importance of vitamins and minerals in correct proportions has been stressed. This aspect is *so very* important.

Iguanas will imprint on many foodstuffs and devour even those with little nutritional value with gusto. To almost all iguana diets, therefore, it will be necessary to add at least two components, calcium and vitamin D_3.

• Calcium is necessary for proper bone development and life itself. Ultraviolet rays allow reptiles to properly metabolize calcium. Natural sunlight is the best source for UV, but full-spectrum lighting provides a little.

• Vitamin D_3 is necessary to help a reptile absorb the necessary calcium. Too much vitamin D_3 will allow too much calcium to be absorbed.

• Phosphorus, present in most foods, can hinder the proper metabolism of calcium.

• Vitamin A, as B carotene is usually present in adequate amounts in the diet of your iguana. Vitamin A enhancements are seldom necessary.

• Vitamin B. Of the various B vitamins, it is only B_1 (thiamine) that may prove a problem to your iguana, and this only if the lizard is allowed to consume plantlife containing the enzyme thiaminase. Thiaminase, contained in many commonly grown house plants, can inhibit the metabolism of vitamin B_1. The B complex vitamins can also be destroyed by medications. If it has been necessary to treat your iguana with antibiotics, the B complex vitamins should be replenished to assure proper digestion.

• Vitamin C is adequately present in balanced diets. A deficiency could manifest itself in hemorrhaging of the mucous membranes and bruising.

• Vitamin D. The integral role of vitamin D_3 in the health of your iguana has already been discussed in detail. The other D complex vitamins seem somewhat less important and are usually present in sufficient amounts.

• Vitamin E deficiencies are diet-related. Feeding your iguana as the herbivore it is will assure that no E vitamin deficiencies occur.

Expelling salt: By sneezing, iguanas expel salts that have been concentrated by specialized glands in their nasal cavities. This is an entirely natural process of salt removal. The expelling of these salts, often first noticed by keepers as crystals around the nostrils of the iguana or on the glass of the terrarium, is not a cause for alarm.

Constipation and Diarrhea

The normal bowel movements of iguanas vary remarkably in consistency. Normal bowel movements are largely brown in coloration with white, chalky urates—much like those a bird produces. Those of a properly hydrated lizard will be moist, almost like a semiliquid jelly. Those of dehydrating specimens will be dry.

Bowel movements *do not* necessarily occur at regular intervals. The body temperature of your lizard will largely determine that speed with which digestion occurs. Cooler lizards will stool less frequently than specimens kept at warmer temperatures.

If an iguana is kept too cool, the digestion process may either stop or be so inhibited that ingested foods spoil in the stomach. In extreme cases, the lizard may vomit these masses. Properly warm temperatures are mandatory for normal and digestive processes to occur. An ideal daytime temperature range would be between 86 and 94°F (30–24.4°C). Slightly cooler daytime temperatures from 77 to 80°F (25–26.7°C) are permissible.

The failure of an iguana to pass stools may also result from a gastrointestinal impaction. The chances of this occurring are heightened in iguanas that are grossly overweight or very inactive. Impactions may be caused by ingested matter (pebbles or kitty litter), or by abnormally dry stools (in under-hydrated iguanas). Again, proper hydration will preclude many problems.

A period of activity, such as a swim in a tub of tepid water, may induce defecation. However, large, immovable impactions may require veterinary intervention. Some impactions may respond to small amounts of softening agents or lubricants available from your pharmacy. Use small amounts of petroleum jelly, milk of magnesia, or Siblin administered orally.

Fecal material that is not expelled has more and more moisture resorbed, and then normal bowel peristaltic motion cannot expel it. These stubborn impactions may require surgical removal.

Diarrhea is a condition in which your iguana produces abnormally loose stools. Occasional loose stools may be induced by a diet change, by the presence of moisture-retaining fruit, by periods of stress, during illness, or other such conditions. In most cases, this is nothing to worry about. Cutting back on fruit and/or adding items with a higher fiber content will likely correct the fecal looseness.

Intestinal worms and abnormally high counts of protozoa can also cause diarrhea. These problems will need to be resolved. The worms should be eradicated. The protozoa count can be lowered via administration of a medication such as Flagyl. Veterinary intervention is indicated in either case. Remember always that some gut-bacteria are necessary to break down the plant cellulose, which is a major component of your iguana's diet.

Pathogens and Parasites

Respiratory ailments: One morning you walk over to your new iguana's cage, carrying a bowl of freshly prepared calcium- and phosphorous-balanced food, and you look at your iguana. Something is wrong. Instead of scurrying over to the cage door, ready to leap atop its food bowl, your iguana is on its hot spot, head down, eyes closed. Its nose is running. Your lizard isn't interested in food. What's happened? What can you do?

Well-acclimated, properly maintained iguanas are not prone to respiratory ailments. But stressed new imports and marginally healthy iguanas and those subjected to unnatural periods of cold (especially humid cold) may occasionally break down with colds or pneumonia. Some respiratory ailments may also be associated with the weakening brought about by an untenably heavy endoparasite burden.

Stress, then, of one kind or another, is usually the culprit to which the origin of a respiratory ailment can be traced. (How many times have you seen someone go through a very stressful time, only to have the burden of a bad cold added to the problems? It happens to iguanas too.)

Here are some suggestions to lessen the possibility of respiratory illness occurring:
• Cage your iguana properly; prevent drafts.
• If kept with a cagemate, iguana or otherwise, be certain all are compatible.
• Have your iguana checked for parasites.
• Keep temperatures within norms at all times.
• In northern climes, have backup heating systems in place.
• Feed your iguana a proper diet.

Respiratory ailments are initially accompanied by sneezing, lethargic demeanor, and unnaturally rapid, often shallow, breathing.

As the respiratory illness worsens, rasping and bubbling may accompany each of your iguana's breaths. At this stage, the respiratory disease is often critical and can be fatal.

The first thing to do is to warm up the basking area. It is essential that basking temperatures be elevated during treatment.

Medical Treatments for Parasitism

Many iguanas, even those that are captive-bred and captive-hatched, may harbor internal parasites. Because of the complexities of identification of endoparasites and the necessity to accurately weigh specimens to be treated as well as to measure dosages, the eradication of internal parasites is best left to a qualified reptile veterinarian. These are a few of the medications and dosages recommended by Richard Funk, D.V.M.

Amoebas and Trichomonads
Metronidazole is given orally at a dosage of 40–50 mg/kg. The treatment is repeated in two weeks.

Dimetridazole can also be used, but the dosage is very different. A dosage of 40–50 mg/kg of dimetrizadole is administered daily for five days. The treatment is then repeated in two weeks. All treatments with both medications are administered once daily.

Coccidia
Sulfadiazine, sulfamerazine and **sulfamethazine** are all given in identical dosages. Administer 75 mg/kg the first day, then follow up for the next five days with 45 mg/kg. All treatments are administered orally and once daily.

Sulfadimethoxine is also effective. The initial dosage is 90 mg/kg orally to be followed on the next five days with 45 mg/kg orally. All dosages are administered once daily.

Trimethoprim-sulfa may also be used. A dosage of 30 mg/kg should be administered once daily for seven days.

Cestodes (Tapeworms)
Bunamidine may be administered orally at a dosage of 50 mg/kg. A second treatment occurs in 14 days.

Niclosamide, orally, at a dosage of 150 mg/kg, is also effective. A second treatment is given in two weeks.

Praziquantel may be administered either orally or intramuscularly. The dosage is 5–8 mg/kg and is to be repeated in 14 days.

Trematodes (Flukes)
Praziquantel at 8 mg/kg may be administered either orally or intramuscularly. The treatment is repeated in two weeks.

Nematodes (Roundworms)

Levamisole, an injectible intraperi-toneal treatment, should be administered at a dosage of 10 mg/kg. The treatment is to be repeated in two weeks.

Ivermectin, injected intramuscularly in a dosage of 200 mcg/kg is effective. The treatment is to be repeated in two weeks. Ivermectin can be toxic to certain taxa.

Thiabendazole and **fenbendazole** have similar dosages. Both are administered orally at 50–100 mg/kg and repeated in 14 days.

Mebendazole is administered orally at a dosage of 20–25 mg/kg and repeated in 14 days.

Iguanas are dependent upon outside heat sources for their metabolic rate. The warmer the surroundings, the better able the iguana is to digest its food, and fight off diseases or injury.

As soon as a respiratory ailment is suspected, elevate the temperature of your iguana's basking area to 96 to 98°F (35.6–36.7°C). (*Do not elevate the temperature of the entire cage to this temperature.*) The ambient cage temperature should be 88 to 92°F (31.1–33.3°C). If the symptoms of respiratory distress do not greatly lessen within a day or two, do not delay any longer. Call your veterinarian and take your iguana to him or her for treatment.

There are many "safe" drugs available, but some respiratory illnesses do not respond well to these. The newer aminoglycoside drugs are more effective, but correspondingly more dangerous. There is little latitude in dosage amounts and the iguana *must* be well hydrated to ensure against renal (kidney) damage. The injection site for aminoglycosides must be *anterior* to mid-body to assure that the renal-portal system is not compromised. It is essential that your veterinarian be well acquainted with reptilian medicine to assure that the correct decisions are made.

Endoparasites: The presence of internal parasites in wild-caught iguanas is a foregone conclusion. Among others that may be present are roundworms, pinworms, nematodes, tapeworms, and a whole host of flagellate protozoans. Although many persons feel blanket treatment of all imported iguanas a necessity, I feel that whether or not the parasites are combated vigorously should depend on the behavior of the iguana itself. Certainly the problems created by endoparasitic loads in weakened iguanas need be addressed promptly. Because fecal exams will have to be run to determine what the iguana is actually harboring in its gut, it is best to avail yourself of the services of a reptilian veterinarian. He or she will be best qualified to determine when and with what to treat the problem.

However, if the specimen in question is bright-eyed, alert, feeding well, and has a good color, you may wish to forgo an immediate veterinary assessment. Endoparasitic burdens can actually diminish if you keep the cage of your specimen scrupulously clean, thereby preventing reinfestation.

Simply stated, the treatment for endoparasites involves administering a poison into the system of your iguana. Because of this, dosages of the drugs *must be EXACT!* It is a very easy matter for a layman who is not familiar with the conversion of the metric doses of medication to overmedicate or undermedicate a patient. In the first case, the result may be fatal. In the latter case, the effort will probably have been futile. Again, I *strongly* suggest you avail yourself of the services of a knowledgeable veterinarian.

Note: Gut and tissue strongylid nematodes are particularly persistent and may require a lengthy bout of treatments to eradicate. I have often wondered at what point a treatment causes more distress for an animal than the problem for which it is being treated. In the case of strongyles, I feel the answer is a toss-up. Whereas an overload of strongyles can cause chronic diarrhea, a potentially debilitating and always unsanitary problem, a small load of these parasites may cause no problems whatever. I feel that discrimination should be used by the veterinarian in determining whether or not to treat the specimen in question. Of course, if the iguana is being treated for other parasite problems anyway, eradication of the strongyles, also, should be accomplished.

Ectoparasites: External parasites are less problematic to treat than endoparasites. Only two kinds, ticks and mites, are seen with any degree of regularity. Both ticks and mites feed on the body fluids of their hosts. Both are easily overlooked.

Ticks are the larger of the two, deflated and seedlike when empty, rounded and bladderlike when engorged. It is best if they are removed singly whenever seen. They imbed their mouthparts deeply when feeding, and if merely pulled from the lizard these may break off in the wound. It is best to first dust them individually with Sevin powder or to rub their body parts with rubbing alcohol, then return a few minutes later and pull the ticks gently off with a pair of tweezers.

Thanks to the advent of Pest Strips (2.2 dichlorovinyl dimethyl phosphate) mites are easily managed. A small square, approximately 0.75×0.75 inches (19×19 mm) placed in the iguana tank (kept out of reach of the lizard) for from 12 to 24 hours will usually kill adult mites. If some survive the initial treatment, treat again a day later. Pest Strips do not destroy mite eggs; therefore it will be necessary to repeat the entire treatment nine days later, when the mite eggs have hatched.

Several other diseases and maladies may more rarely befall your pet iguana. Among these are:
• Mineralization of internal organs: This is caused by oversupplementation of calcium. Known as hypercalcemia, a treatment has been developed. The treatment is both lengthy and expensive, requiring about two weeks of monitoring by a veterinarian. There is a fine line between enough and too much calcium and vitamin D_3. Once diagnosed and corrected, it will be necessary for you to reduce both calcium and vitamin D_3 intake by your specimen. If untreated or too far advanced, this can be a fatal problem. (See Frye, F.L. and W. Townsend, *Iguanas: A Guide to Their Biology and Captive Care.*)
• Hypoglycemia relates to low blood sugar. Stress or pancreatic dysfunction can be the causative agent. The stress factor is correctable; the pancreatic dysfunction, most commonly caused by an insulin-secreting tumor, usually is not.
• Diabetes is also caused by pancreatic dysfunction. As in diabetic humans, a program of regular and continuing insulin injections can be undertaken. The alternative is euthanasia.
• Herpes virus has been found to exist in green iguanas. When diagnosed, euthanasia of the lizard is recommended.

Mechanical Injury

Despite the best care you can give, sometimes iguanas are injured. They can find a way to lodge themselves between a heating lamp and the enclosure, and get burned; a staple may break off and the jagged edge may cut the iguana; the lizard may get injured in the shipping process en route to the pet store. With animals, as with small children, you can adopt a corollary of Murphy's Law: they can get hurt when you least expect it.

This section deals with injuries, such as burns, cuts and abrasions, injured toes, broken tails and limbs, and skin shedding problems.

Burns: Your captive iguana can be burned in any of several ways. The most frequent of these involves your lizard being in prolonged contact with a cage heating or lighting element that is either malfunctioning or for which a proper protective device has not been installed.

Among others, hot rocks, other heating units, and incandescent lightbulbs have been implicated in superficial to severe burning incidents.

Burned areas are often discolored but usually not blistered. Treatment will depend upon the severity of the burn. Superficial burns will often require no treatment at all, but the causative agent must, of course, be modified, buffered, or removed. Moderate burns will need to be cleaned and antiseptic ointment applied, especially if there are suppurations. Severe burns will need vigorous medical treatment and your veterinarian should be consulted immediately. One of the problems you will encounter is the appetite loss of the animal, combined with a great need for fluids and energy and calories for healing.

I am not a proponent of hot rocks or heat bricks or other similar ventrally oriented heating devices. Iguanas (and other basking species) are usually heliothermic animals. They thermoregulate by basking in the sunlight until warm, then move to a more shaded area so as not to overheat. They are designed to most efficiently absorb and evenly distribute warmth through their bodies when heated from above. This should not be construed as meaning that on cloudy days, or even at other times when they are cool, they will not happily rest on a warmed surface. They will! It is just that they are not usually forced to do so on a regular basis. Because of this dorsal orientation, I feel it is much more natural if your lizard is heated from *above*, and apparently the lizards feel the same way. Iguanas (and other heliotherms) will usually more readily and regularly utilize a lighted area warmed by a heat bulb than the nonilluminated, ventrally oriented hot rocks with which they are so often supplied.

Heat and other incandescent bulbs will need to be carefully placed, too. Burns from a high wattage, heat-emitting bulb are even more possible than from hot rocks.

Cuts and abrasions: Cuts and abrasions may be as diverse as burns in severity. The seriousness of either will determine the response necessary by you. The cause of the injury will need to be immediately corrected. If the wound is dirty, you'll need to clean it with soap and water (be sure to rinse well). For the more minimal of these problems, an over-the-counter antiseptic ointment will suffice. As with humans, if possible, the area needs to be protected from dirt until it heals. The problem is that commercial adhesive gauze strips either won't stick to iguana skin or they stick too well and you'll have problems in removal. Depending on where the injury is, you might be able to wrap a gauze bandage around the affected area, and secure the bandage to itself with adhesive tape or the adhesive elastic bandage. For the more serious wounds, veterinary assistance should be immediately sought.

Nose rubbing: One of the most common causes of abrasion is also one of the most difficult to correct. This is nose rubbing. It is the direct result of escape efforts by your iguana and may be indulged in by either tame or wild specimens. Whether the cage is of glass or wire (smooth or rough) construction makes little difference.

Nose rubbing by newly caged iguanas that have been used to "the run

Larger iguanas are particularly subject to trauma on their snouts, simply because the larger lizards frighten more easily.

of the house" is self-explanatory. Nose rubbing by fearful wild iguanas that are trying unsuccessfully to return to the wild iguanas is equally easily explained.

Methods for lessening the problem include providing larger cages, a greater feeling of security, and more actual "freedom." Often, covering at least three sides of the cage with opaque paper, cloth, or "contact paper" may alleviate or curtail the problem.

To prevent easily startled, extremely wild, specimens from repeatedly reinjuring their snouts, it may be necessary to also cover the remaining side. However, in truth this is self-defeating, for it will prevent the iguana ever becoming accustomed to motion and your presence. Another method, one that I prefer for extremely wild specimens, is to suspend a soft cloth barrier 2 or so inches (about 5 cm) on the *inside* of the glass or wire sides of the cage. By coming in contact with the hanging cloth first, the iguana substantially lessens its impact with the cage side. For the open side of the cage, the side that you approach most frequently, the barricade can be suspended from the center on down. This way, the lizard can see you and yet avoid injury if it runs into the cage wall.

Toe problems: Broken toes, torn-off toenails, and sharp claws are all frequently encountered when one works with or keeps iguanas (or, indeed, almost any other lizard).

Toes may be broken during escape efforts, or if the iguana catches its claws inextricably in constrictions offered by carpeting or a narrow aperture. Sometimes humans cause this by stepping on the toe of a loose iguana. If the break is fresh and simple, the toe may often be splinted and saved. If the break is old and/or compound, amputation is usually preferred. Consult your veterinarian.

Torn-off toenails occur for the same series of reasons that breaks do.

Merely apply an antiseptic ointment or powder and keep your iguana quiet until the bleeding stops. These will often heal quickly without any additional procedures being necessary. However, if the toe becomes infected, consult your veterinarian.

Iguanas of most kinds display arboreal propensities in the wild. To accommodate their climbing habits, their claws are sharp and recurved. In the wild, the normal activity pattern of the lizard usually keeps the claws somewhat dulled. Because most captive iguanas never have the opportunity to climb and run extensively, it may be desirable to occasionally clip off the very tip of the claw. Often a two-person job, nail trimming is easiest (especially if the iguana is large) if the specimen is firmly but gently restrained and rolled onto its side with its belly facing the person who is to do the trimming. Using either human or pet nail clippers, it is then possible to remove the claw tip. If the claws of

Darkened and sunken eyes, faded colors and a listless mien indicate a seriously ill iguana.

baby iguanas are carefully inspected, it is often possible to see traces of venation at their cores. Care should be taken *not* to cut the claw so short that it bleeds. If bleeding does occur, apply a styptic or an antibiotic powder.

Occasionally a constriction of fiber or even unshed skin on the toe can inhibit normal blood circulation. If unresolved, this can lead to the distal portion blackening as the tissue dies, dries out, and eventually drops off. Normally this is not accompanied by any swelling or infection, and, in fact, is seldom detected until it is too late to correct the problem. A periodic inspection of your iguana's toes for constricting fibers or rings of dried skin, and their prompt and gentle removal if found, can lessen the probability of this occurring.

Broken tails: Although the breaking of a tail in an otherwise perfect specimen of iguana can be disheartening, the occurrence quite probably affects the keeper more profoundly than the kept. The tails of iguanas (and most other lizards) are designed by Mother Nature to break if necessary. In fact, the tail structure of some lizard species is so delicate that autotomization (breaking) will occur at a mere touch. This is a defensive mechanism with considerable survival value. In each of the caudal (tail) vertebrae there is a weakened "fracture plane" to facilitate easy breakage. If, as frequently does happen, a predator grasps the lizard by the tail, the tail breaks off and through convulsive wriggling, retains the predator's attention. Little bleeding accompanies the autotomization, and regeneration of the tail begins immediately. The completeness and appearance depends upon numerous criteria. Among others are the age of the lizard, the area of the break, and whether or not the break was clean and complete or irregular and partial.

Tails broken halfway or more of the way back usually regenerate more

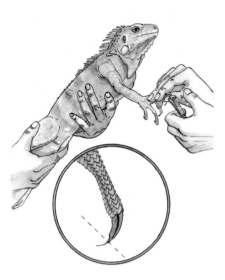

Only the very tip of the claw should be trimmed.

completely than those broken closer to the body. A clean, complete break will usually result in a more normally tapering, natural appearing regenerated member. With care (and luck), a partial break may heal in a natural position. Alternatively, the break may complete itself at a later date or heal askew. In some cases, a second, abnormal appearing tail may grow to join the first.

Tails of young iguanas broken on their distal half seldom need attention. Tails of adult iguanas broken on their distal one third are likewise not apt to require attention. The tails of both young and old broken closer to the body may require cauterization and/or suturing to staunch blood flow and quickly close the wound.

Broken limbs: The leg bones of an iguana are strong and designed to withstand more than considerable stress without mishap. In the wild, an

If untreated, toe infections can lead to toe loss.

52

iguana with a broken limb would be easy prey in a predator strewn habitat. Green iguanas have been seen to drop several dozen feet from a tree limb where they were basking to both dry ground and water. After landing on the former they scuttled off at considerable speed, showing no evidence that the drop had affected them adversely. When landing in water they dive and swim to safety, again showing no ill effects from the considerable landing impact.

Therefore, if a captive iguana breaks its leg, it is *usually* the cause of either an accident or indicative of another underlying problem such as metabolic bone disease. In either case, splinting (and/or pinning, depending upon the severity and complexity of the break) will be necessary. Veterinary help should be sought immediately.

If the break was the cause of an accident, steps should be taken to ascertain that it does not have an opportunity to recur. If it is determined that the break was the result of calcium deficiency, the condition should be first stabilized with injectable calcium and then dietary corrections should be immediately made.

Infections: If kept clean, iguanas are not likely to develop infections, even from open wounds. It is when their quarters are allowed to become dirty, or when the animals are stressed, that infections are most likely to occur. If untreated, infections can literally overwhelm even an otherwise healthy iguana in a rather short time.

Abscesses, suppurations, discolorations, and other such abnormal signs may indicate either a localized or a systemic infection. Swollen limbs can also mean metabolic bone disease (see page 42), an equally serious problem. A veterinarian well versed in reptilian disorders should be consulted

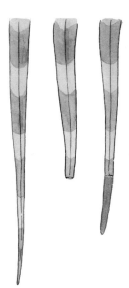

The regenerated tip (right) of a broken tail (center) is never as perfect as the original (left).

immediately. In some cases it may be necessary to run cultures to determine an efficacious treatment. In other cases the causative agents may respond quickly to broad-spectrum antibiotics (these will usually be injected for immediate action. When an iguana is this sick, it generally doesn't eat and has trouble metabolizing the food it does eat.) In all cases, proper cleanliness of both lizard and cage are essential.

Shedding "problems": An iguana that walks around sporting large patches of exfoliating skin is apt to be perceived as an iguana with problems. Such is not usually the case.

Reptiles shed their skin to facilitate growth. This is natural. Unlike snakes, which are well known for their entire, inverted shed skins, most lizards shed their skin less neatly and in a patchwork manner. This, too, is natural—unless the skin adheres tightly and is not lost by the lizard within a day or two. Increasing the humidity in the iguana cage and moistening your lizard's shedding skin will often help to dislodge it. A gentle tug by you on the edges may also help. It is important, however, that you do not remove the flaking skin before it is ready to be removed. The newly forming skin beneath it may be damaged if things are rushed.

Do spend a few moments checking your iguana over after each shed. Ascertain that no rings of scales remain on the digits, tail, or elsewhere, where they may then dry and restrict circulation. Should you find such problems, remove the skin gently and promptly. It

Medical abbreviations
mg —milligram
(1 mg = 0.001 gram)
kg —kilogram
(1000 grams; 2.2 pounds)
mcg —microgram
(1 mcg = 0.000001 gram)
IM —intramuscularly
IP —intraperitoneally
PO —orally

may be necessary to soak your iguana for a few minutes first to promote softening and facilitate the easy removal.

Clear eyes and good color equate to good health.

54

Reproduction

Although many persons consider merely keeping an iguana hale and hearty a sufficient challenge, there is, among iguana keepers, an ever-increasing number who wish to breed their lizards. Successful reproduction in captivity is a confirmation that the husbandry techniques being used are as good or better than natural conditions.

To breed your iguanas you—and they—need to ascertain and meet several criteria. The most important of these, of course, is to have a pair; a male and a female iguana old and large enough to breed. It is also necessary to have provided caging large enough to permit courtship and an egg deposition site.

The lizards will probably be large enough if they are two-thirds or more grown (females, 3 feet [0.9 m] or more, and males, 4 feet [1.2 m] or more in length—the almost-to-fully-grown males are considerably larger than the females of equal age). The pair also needs to be compatible, as well as happy and healthy enough to breed.

Once successfully bred, the female needs to have a deposition chamber in which to lay her clutch. Lastly, you need the knowledge and facilities to hatch those viable eggs that are laid. Certainly there is a ready market for those captive-bred young, as an alternative to the taking of specimens from the wild.

Breeding Basics

Although not easy, if compatible iguanas are kept in large enough facilities and are "cycled" properly, successfully breeding is far from impossible. The term "cycle," as used here, pertains to the factors (climatic, light duration, and others) that must be controlled to ready your iguanas for breeding.

The breeding sequences of most reptiles and amphibians are at least partially triggered by external stimuli. Prominent among these stimuli are seasonal temperature changes, seasonal humidity changes, and photoperiods. Indeed, many temperate climate reptiles cannot be successfully bred unless they are subjected to a period of cooling and darkness similar to that which occurs during their periods of brumation (reptile/amphibian hibernation).

Green iguanas are tropical creatures that do not undergo extended periods of dormancy. But even in their southern haunts, they experience certain annual climatic changes. For the more northerly ranging iguanas, these changes include slightly reduced hours of winter daylight, slightly lowered winter nighttime temperatures, reduced winter relative humidity, and a lessening of rain activity during the winter months. The climatic changes are even less in the more tropical areas, being largely limited to a reduction of humidity and shower activity during the winter months. Slight though these changes may be, they play a profound role in the life cycle of the green iguana. You can reproduce these natural conditions by adhering to a natural photoperiod (turn your lights on and off with sunrise and sunset, or use a timer and increase day length with the lengthening days after

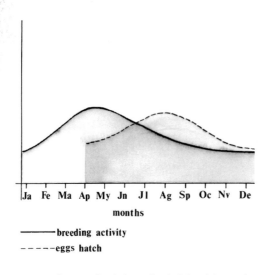

Ja Fe Ma Ap My Jn Jl Ag Sp Oc Nv De

months

———— breeding activity

- - - - eggs hatch

Iguanas begin breeding in late winter and the eggs begin hatching a few months later.

the winter solstice); adding spring "rain showers," and keeping nighttime temperatures slightly lower than daytime temperatures.

The periods of reduced light, temperature, humidity, and rainfall that occur from late winter to very early spring trigger a hormonal decrease that results in ovarian and testicular regression. The reproductive urge is absent. With the lengthening days and correspondingly increasing warmth, humidity, and rain activity of spring and summer, hormonal production again increases. The testicles and ovaries resume production, interest in reproduction picks up, and iguana-to-iguana interaction becomes a matter of territory, fighting, and sex.

Male Rivalry

Male iguanas that had previously shared the same caging arrangement will now view each other as rivals. It is at this time that what may have until then been compatible groups of iguanas are apt to become

quarrelsome. You'll need to provide some type of separation between males, because they won't remember who won the last fight; if they encounter each other, they will fight. This sort of single-mindedness will take precedence over normal activities such as sunning or feeding, and is stressful both for the victor and the loser, although more so, of course, for the latter.

Courtship

If the two iguanas are male and female, courtship will begin. The possibilities for courtship will be enhanced if the lizards have been separated from each other, even if only for a week or so, and then "reintroduced."

The courtship of a female iguana by a male is characterized by stylized body language (rather similar to that used in territoriality displays). The courtship involves push-ups, head bobs and nods, and repeated dewlap distensions. The female may or may not respond by bobbing and push-ups; her own response is more subtle and is accomplished by her presence (she leaves if she isn't interested) and through scent. The females produce pheromones, scented "signals" that indicate willingness to breed. Males, of course, recognize these scent cues and respond accordingly.

After the whirlwind courtship the male will mount the female, retaining position by grasping her nape with his jaws. The male will curve and angle his body around that of the female until cloacae are juxtaposed. When their bodies are correctly positioned, intromission is usually quickly accomplished and is accompanied by a varied series of movements, including a "shrugging" sequence. After breeding is completed, the iguanas again go their separate ways.

Throughout late winter and early spring months, iguanas are opportunistic breeders. Although they may mate later in the year, those breedings that seem most successful occur between January and May. Being largely loners, when the paths of two receptive iguanas of the opposite sex cross during those months, more often than not, they will breed.

Nesting

Eggs will be laid about 60 to 65 days later, in an area the female has carefully chosen and just as carefully prepared. After choosing a suitable site, she will use her forefeet to dig deeply into the earth. Loosened dirt and debris will be removed with the rear feet. She will excavate until the hole is sufficiently large for her to enter and be completely secluded during the egg laying. Usually, several times during preparations, the female will reverse her head-down position and peer quizzically from the deepening depression, perhaps scouting for approaching danger. Certainly at this time, while her head is down in a constraining hole, she is more vulnerable to predation than at almost any other time in her adult life.

The nesting efforts may be curtailed at any time during the preparation. If disturbed by a predator or if the digging is thwarted by a maze of roots or rocks, the female will often leave to begin anew elsewhere at another time. Even if completed after several periods of digging interspersed with periods of rest, the female, based upon criteria known best to her, may deem the nesting chamber unsuitable. Should this be the case, the female will abandon the completed but unused nest and proceed to excavate at another location and another time.

However, if all is deemed well with the initial excavation, the female will, after a period of rest, lay and position anywhere from 10 to 55 eggs, then fill the hole with the removed dirt, and leave. Left in place in a warm climate, and dependent on temperature and moisture, the period of incubation can and will vary considerably. At the low end, under ideal nest conditions, the eggs may hatch in about 70 days. Under cooler, dryer conditions the incubation duration may near a full three months.

In Dade County, Florida, feral iguanas have been seen breeding (temperatures allowing) from early mid-February to late May. Nesting activities have been noted in the months of April, May, June, and July. Hatchlings have been found throughout the calendar months of summer. In that seasonally dry, almost xeric area, females tend to construct their nests beneath moisture-containing roadside trash. Recently, an egg-laden female was found during nest construction beneath a discarded damp mattress.

Iguanas breed somewhat earlier in their native Latin America than in Florida, and imported, captive-bred hatchlings begin flooding the pet markets in June.

Breeding Iguanas

To breed iguanas you will need, of course, a mature pair. Males have a larger head, a larger crest, a larger dewlap, proportionately larger femoral pores, and a more massive build. Iguanas that are "tame," content in captivity, and healthy make the best breeders. If your iguanas are fearful and skittish, breeding sequences are easily interrupted. Allow your female to become accustomed to the nesting chamber, prior to egg deposition.

The Incubation Process

Once the eggs have been laid and the female has covered the eggs with the nesting material and departed, you need to remove the eggs and incubate them. Expect to find 10 to 55 eggs

A hatching baby green iguana will look out-side its egg several times before emerging.

Making Your Own Incubator

You'll need:
- a thermostat/heater (available from feed stores)
- a thermometer
- a Styrofoam cooler—one with thick sides (a fish shipping box is ideal)

Poke a hole through the lid of the Styrofoam cooler, and suspend the thermostat/heater from the inside. Add another hole for a thermome-ter, so you can check on the inside temperature without opening the top. If there's no flange on the ther-mometer to keep it from slipping through the hole in the lid, use a rubber band wound several times around the thermometer to form a flange.

Put the lid on the cooler, and plug in the thermostat/heater. Wait half an hour and check the temperature. Adjust the thermostat/ heater until the temperature inside the incuba-tor is about 86°F (30°C).

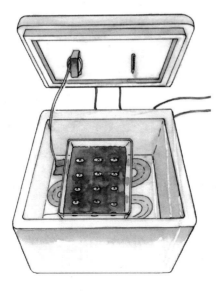

Home-made incubators are easily con-structed and serve well.

(some clutches contain 80!), oval in shape with a soft, parchmentlike shell. Each egg is about 1.5 by 1 inches, (38.1 × 25.4 mm).

You'll place the eggs in a series of containers, which in turn will be placed inside the incubator. Incubation is a simple but exacting process that involves keeping the eggs at the proper warmth and humidity.

Make sure that you do not turn the eggs as you move them. If it would help, use a pencil to make an "x" on the top side of each egg before you move it, so you'll know where the top is. With reptile eggs, the position of the air pocket inside the egg cannot change, once the egg has been laid. If the egg is "rolled over," the air pocket moves and the embryo suffocates.

Place the eggs in a series of plastic sweater or shoe boxes that have been

58

filled halfway with dampened vermic-ulite. Make a depression in the sur-face of the vermiculite for each egg, and do not let the eggs touch each other. Cover the filled boxes and put them inside the incubator.

You can rent a chicken incubator for the period of incubation, roughly 60 to 86 days, or you buy one from a feed store. You can also make your own from a good-sized Styrofoam cooler and a thermostat/heater and a thermometer.

You'll need to monitor both the tem-perature and the humidity. The pre-ferred humidity is 100 percent, which can be accomplished by keeping the hatching medium of peat and soil damp to the touch but too dry to squeeze out any water when squeezed by your hand. The normal temperature range for iguana egg incubation in the wild is 82 to 90°F (27.8–32.2°C), with 85 to 87°F (29.4–30.6°C) the preferred temperature.

Once you have the temperature reg-ulated, put the shoe/sweater box con-taining the eggs inside the incubator and close the lid. Check the tempera-ture daily and add a little water to the incubating medium as needed. You'll

need to remove the eggs with obvious problems, like fuzzy mold, but because the eggs aren't touching each other, the other eggs won't be spoiled.

How do you know if the eggs are fertile? By the end of the first week, those eggs that are not fertile will turn yellow, harden, and begin to collapse. Those that are fertile will remain white and turgid to the touch. Infertile eggs should be removed and thrown away.

At the end of 60 to 85 days, if all goes well, your baby iguanas will begin to "pip" their eggs. Iguanas in the egg bear a small egg tooth (called a caruncle) on the tip of their snout, which they use to slit the egg.

The babies are really in no hurry to leave the egg. They will cut a slit, look out, and decide to stay inside the egg for a while longer, perhaps as long as a day and a half. Eventually each egg that has matured enough to hatch, will. The live babies will emerge from the eggs and can be removed to another terrarium and offered food, a sunning spot, and water. (If any eggs remain un-pipped, continue to incu-bate them until they go bad.)

Congratulations on your new babies!

Few lizards are as appealing as a baby green iguana.

HOW-TO:
Preparing the Nesting Site

Iguanas kept out-of-doors in the southernmost areas of the United States and other areas where winters are mild, can be allowed to breed and nest nearly as they would in the wild. You, as an owner, merely need to ascertain that suitable nesting areas are present in the cages. For outdoor enclosures that rest directly upon the ground, the female iguana will construct her own nest in much the way she would in the wild. If she does not begin her own nest (and you feel the substrate is suitable), merely disturbing the surface of the ground may be an adequate prompt.

The Outdoor Enclosure

Occasionally a female can be induced to nest by providing her with a darkened nesting chamber. Suitability seems governed by four considerations: adequate amounts of space and darkness as well as appropriate moisture content and proper temperature.

An "in-ground" nest can easily be made by digging down and framing (on the sides only—the bottom must be left uncovered for the female to dig and deposit the eggs) an adequately sized depression. An entryway must be left open, of course. Finally, it will be necessary to cover the wooden chamber with a piece of plywood or other suitably opaque top. The gravid female iguana may either deposit her eggs in this chamber exactly as provided, or she may scratch an additional depression in the dirt that the nesting box covers. Once the eggs are laid, she will cover them with loose soil.

Alternatively, you could go to your local hardware store and purchase a large plastic trash or garbage can; the size can range from 44 to 60 gallons (166.6–227 L). Choose one that is dark brown or dark green; a female iguana will be more inclined to deposit her eggs in an area she feels is safest, and she'll feel safest where it's dark. A round can will be fine for an outdoor enclosure, because you can sink it into the ground to anchor it.

Use a serrated knife, a hacksaw, or a jigsaw to cut off the bottom one third of the trash can. This bottom piece will form the basic nest enclosure. (If the cut edge seems rough, use a file or 200-grit sandpaper to smooth the edge.) Turn the piece over so the bottom is uppermost. Cut an entry hole near the top, large enough to permit easy entry by the female, 6 to 8 inches (15.2–20.3 cm) in diameter, and smooth the edges. Place the nest box in the iguana cage, burying the edge in the ground to secure it. You only want to leave about 8 to 10 inches (20.3–25.4 cm) of the top of the nest box above the ground. Leave the surface of the soil inside the box disturbed, to facilitate the digging by the female.

You may decide to join forces with those breeders who feel the nesting site should be very secluded, to the point of providing an underground entranceway to the chamber. Such entrance-

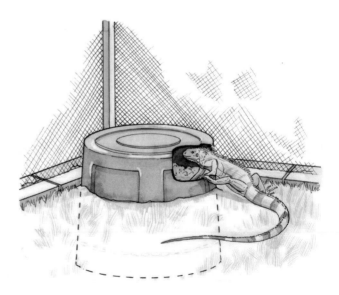

An excellent nesting chamber for an iguana may be made from the bottom third of a plastic trash can.

This nesting chamber has an underground access.

its side. Cut an entry hole for the female in one of the corners of the lid, about 6 to 8 inches (15.2–20.3 cm) in diameter. Fill the can halfway with a mixture of moistened soil, and sand. A little peat moss can be mixed in to help retain moisture and lighten the nesting medium.

Tape the lid securely onto the trash can, and place your newly constructed nesting box in the iguana cage. Put it on one of its broad sides, with the entry hole uppermost. The nesting medium should form a layer that halfway fills the can. Secure the nesting box by sliding it into a corner of the cage where the can will not over heat.

This trash can set-up may also be used successfully in outdoor cages.

ways are certainly not mandatory. However, should you decide to provide one, it is easily made by burying one or more lengths of ceramic pipe of suitable diameter (end to end if more than a single piece is used), sloping them from the surface to the subsurface entrance of the main nesting chamber.

Whether the entrance is via a hole in the nesting box, or an underground entranceway, moistening the ground inside the chamber or box may help encourage the female. If all goes well, she will enter the nest box, recognize it as a good spot to lay her eggs, and will begin digging. After she deposits her eggs in the pit she digs, she will cover the eggs with the loose dirt. Her task is done, and she will leave the nest site. You will need to remove the eggs and incubate them.

The Indoor Enclosure

For an indoor enclosure, purchase a rectangular trash can. Instead of cutting it, you'll use the entire can, placed on

Indoor nesting chambers may be made from a rectangular plastic trash can with an entry hole cut in the lid.

Iguana Watching

Birders have turned bird-watching into a science, and their observation techniques pay off handsomely for those who wish to observe iguanas in the wild. And those "wilds" aren't far off—now, due to accidental or purposeful releases, wild green iguanas can be found in Florida, Texas, and Hawaii. All you need is good eyesight (or a pair of binoculars) and patience.

You can seek out these lizards for field observations and photographs without concerning yourself about permits. If you proceed onto private land, it's just courtesy to ask permission.

The Green Iguana

A recent trip to Miami divulged thriving populations of green iguanas and some other introduced iguana species as well. We had heard about the sighting for years, and so one weekend Florida herpetologist Walter Meshaka and I headed for that city, camera and binoculars in hand.

We walked slowly through the gates of a public garden on Key Biscayne. We were looking for signs of a population of green iguanas. (Miami, being a subtropical area, not only stays warm enough year-round to keep these cold-sensitive lizards active, but the warmer temperatures mean year-round food, as well.)

As we entered the park, a large South American whiptailed lizard darted to cover ahead of us. Interesting, but not our "prey" at this point. At the far end of the gardens, we paralleled a series of freshwater canals. It was there we found them.

The first green iguana was foraging along a canal bank, apparently consuming the fallen fruit from the palm commonly known as "cocos plumosa."

The lizard was a fairly large, adult animal (somewhere in the length range of 4.5 feet [1.4 m]) and its high crest and heavy jowls identified it as a male. Its body coloring was just on the green side of gray, but it shaded to a pale orange on the back and had more brilliant orange (alternating with black) in its crest. It was wary and alert.

We were immediately identified by the animal as "dangerous beings" and it cascaded in headlong flight into some low trees that overhung the canal. Then, knowing it was secure, the lizard allowed us fairly close approach. However, the lighting was so poor that no photos of the lizard were possible.

The second iguana saw us long before we saw it. We heard a crashing through the shrubbery, and by the time we got to the canal bank all that could be seen were an expanding circle of ripples and a school of disturbed fish. Then, as we stood, from halfway across the canal an iguana head emerged from underwater and soon we could see a 5-foot (1.5 m) iguana sculling slowly away from us, peering back toward us as the distance between him and us increased. Upon reaching the distant bank the big lizard clambered out, momentarily paused, then disappeared into the safety and seclusion of a clump of spiny date palms. We did not see it again. We had hit pay dirt.

Green iguanas are by no means confined to these two areas. In fact, they seem even more common in the brushy suburban areas surrounding the Miami International Airport. Recently a large, very gravid female was found there in the act of constructing a nesting chamber beneath an old mattress. Taken captive, she produced a clutch of healthy eggs and was then placed in a breeding program. A second female was taken under similar circumstances only a few days later, she, too, producing a large clutch of viable eggs. Naturally, considering the traffic hazards alone in that general area, not all of the babies would survive to maturity. But the Miami area is certainly home to several generations of these adaptable green lizards.

Now firmly established in the United States, green iguanas can be found in Texas, Hawaii and Florida. You will need patience, sharp eyes, bincoulars, and good luck for iguana watching.

But the green iguana was not all we would see that day. Fifty yards distant, partially shrouded by a patch of huge lilies, lay a cluster of sizable limestone boulders. Atop the largest one was an elongate, slightly raised, black patch. I raised my telephoto lens, hoping that the magnification provided would allow me to discern exactly what that black patch was. I had my suspicions, but still….

It had been thirty years since I had last been in Miami's Crandon Park. It had then been Crandon Park Zoo and I had been a keeper there. The reptile collection was housed in a small, glass-fronted, wooden house. Although extreme care was taken to assure the secure caging of the snakes, there were turtles, tortoises, and many lizards kept in open-topped pits and open-topped walled enclosures. Among those lizards so kept were green iguanas, and Mexican spiny-tailed iguanas (*Ctenosaura pectinata*). Once in a while one or more of the lizards would escape, but because a constant procession of them were brought to us by owners grown tired of their reptilian charges, exact head count was a little sketchy.

The same attitude prevailed at the next key inward. There, in the "Lost Islands" display of the Miami

This spiny-tailed iguana paused just long enough to permit me one photo.

Seaquarium, dwelt numerous big green iguanas and a lesser number of rhinoceros iguanas (*Cyclura cornuta*). Those thirty years ago, with Jerry Fine as my partner, I used to look for both species along the seaquarium's seawall, an area where because of ample cover, escapees could sometimes be seen. Interestingly, there were always at least a few young of each present, but in those days no one gave much thought to the possible ecological impact of establishing alien reptile species.

Less prolific than the green iguanas, rhino iguanas were soon collected out, but green iguanas became increasingly common. And a few years after the sighting of the last rhino iguana there, a new species became established. This was the Mexican spiny-tail, then considered far more exotic than either the rhinos or the green iguanas. Evidently as fecund as the green iguanas, it soon became apparent that the spiny-tail population was also on the increase.

But soon I moved from the Miami area and the iguana populations were quickly forgotten. They remained so for about twenty years. I would see occasional mention of an iguana of some sort being captured in South Florida, but it was not until I began compiling a few statistics on Florida's established alien herpetofauna that the iguanas again became of interest. What, I wondered, had become of colonies of green iguanas (and their cousins) in the thirty-plus intervening years?

...We moved slowly towards the boulders. Finally I raised the camera and through the lens saw that the black patch was actually a magnificent adult male Mexican spiny-tailed iguana. He looked to be about 3.5 feet (1 m) long, and as bulky and as arrogant as most good-sized male lizards.

I was amazed at the sighting, but I shouldn't have been for Walt had told me that the species was actually rather common there. I sidled closer,

approaching obliquely and attempting not to make eye contact with the big lizard (establishing eye contact is one of the surest ways to "spook" any lizard). But it was wary (that's how you get to be a big iguana) and long before I got close enough for a "frame-filler," the iguana clambered over the side of the rock and into a nearby drainage pipe.

We continued on and within moments had found another three adults and a couple of babies. Spiny-tails were indeed common, but *all* were exceedingly wary. Even with a 400-mm lens I didn't really get a suitable picture of any. For us, it was enough to know that the green iguana and one of its relatives were firmly established in south Florida.

If you'd like to do some green iguana watching in the western half of the United States, head for Texas. Reports of feral green iguanas are common from the lower Rio Grande Valley. You can add other iguana species to your "life list" in New Mexico, Utah, California, or Arizona. These states are the homelands of the desert iguanas and chuckwallas; spiny-tails exist in a free state on the grounds of the Arizona-Sonora Desert Museum in Tucson.

Generally speaking, the farther out from civilization you get, the better the lizard watching will be. Be prepared for some warm temperatures; these creatures *like* it hot.

The Chuckwallas

The heat from the lowering desert sun still beat mercilessly from the western sky. Spiny lizards sought respite from the unrelenting warmth in the shadows of saguaro cacti. The long red rays of the sun lent a touch of surrealism to the surrounding rocky ledges. A friend and I were returning to Ajo, Arizona after a day of trying to photograph desert lizards and snakes. We had spent considerable time at

Quitobaquito Spring in Organ Pipe National Monument hoping to photograph Sonoran mud turtles in a natural habitat. We had failed. But failing at photographing was nothing new to us, and success at this pursuit really wasn't as important as just seeing the animals (we had succeeded in that) and adding some natural history lore to our accumulating herpetological knowledge. Quitobaquito had provided us with hours of enjoyment.

Our drive to Quitobaquito had been punctuated with stops and side trips to afford us more opportunity to observe herpetofauna. At many stops we had found that we were the observed long before becoming the observers. Lizards—*big* lizards—were watching our every move. Even before we dragged out the binoculars to ascertain their identifications, we instinctively knew from stance and size these lizards were chuckwallas—"desert chickens" or, simply, "chucks."

And it looked as if our return drive would be an instant replay. As we drove we could see the big lizards sprawled, but attentive, atop rocks both distant and near. When we began to slow they would become more watchful and by the time we had stopped, all had disappeared from sight.

Finally we were motoring a stretch of road where low, stratified, heavily creviced ledges had converged closely on both sides. And with the roadside ledges had come roadside chucks.

Tom Tyning, a naturalist from Massachusetts, slowed the car to hardly more than a crawl. Ahead a chuck sat watching us only a few yards from the road. We neared. He disappeared.

Another chuck; this one atop a ledge that came right to the pavement. We neared, he became alert, but stayed. We parked. He sidled to the edge of the cut—but still he stayed. This was one confidant chuck!

But finally even he had had enough. As we moved slowly toward him, cameras ready, he slowly crawled into a crevice, turned, and looked back out at us. We were able to get a number of photos of "chuck in crevice." On the whole trip this was the *only* chuck that cooperated with us in our photo attempts!

Checking the range map in your field guide will inform you that it was alert specimens of the Arizona chuckwalla (*S. o. tumidus*) that were watching us so intently. They were wary.

How Many Kinds of Chuckwallas Are There?

How many species of these big, waddling, pot-bellied lizards are there? Well, the number will vary from two to six, depending on which authority is quoted. Some researchers consider the form found in the United States, *Sauromalus obesus*, one species, and all others subspecies of the Mexican *S. ater*. Other researchers consider the insular Mexican forms—*ater, hispidus, sleveni,* and *varius*—all separate species. Still others think all the chucks, including the one of the United States, variable races of *S. varius*. The chuck of the southern Baja Peninsula may be referred to by some as *S. australis* (a full species), by other researchers as *S. ater australis* (a subspecies of the insular *S. ater*) and by still other taxonomists as *S. obesus australis* (a subspecies of our own *S. obesus*). Confusing? Only to us. The chucks don't care. They just want to be left alone.

For purposes here, I will consider all except two of the chucks full species: *S. obesus* and *S. ater* are subspeciated.

Chuckwallas are wary enough to seek refuge in rock crevices when people are around.

Even from binocular distance, almost as soon as we turned to scan them, the lizards scuttled out of sight. We began to wonder whether we were ever going to be able to get a sighting that would allow us a positive identification. And, indeed, until meeting the cooperative chuck mentioned in the lead-in, our efforts were for naught.

Sauromalus obesus, the chuckwalla of the deserts of the southwestern United States, is represented here by three subspecies, and in western Sonora and Guaymas Mexico by one. The Sonoran race is designated as *S. o. townsendi*. Even adult males are of duller coloration (lacking most, if not all, of the red pigment) and marginally smaller size than the Arizona race, whose range it abuts.

S. o. tumidus, the Arizona chuck, ranges from central to extreme southwestern Arizona. It also hops the border, being found in adjacent Mexico (extreme northern Sonora). It is a magnificent animal (described above) and has fewer than 50 tiny scales

encircling the mid-forearm. This is a rather prominently tricolored subspecies. The head, shoulders, and forelimbs are black, the torso is brick-red, the rear limbs are dark (hind feet can be light), and the tail is cream.

The western chuckwalla (*S. o. obesus*), a race with a tremendous range, is geographically variable in color. Found from southwest Utah westward across south Nevada to east central California, the range of this big lizard then extends southward, including all of western Arizona and the northern Baja Peninsula. Adult males we saw in southern California were rather similar in appearance to the Arizona chuck, but the red of the torso seemed paler and rather heavily infiltrated with poorly defined darker areas. A spectacular phase of this lizard occurs near Phoenix. In that area, the entire head, all limbs, and torso are jet black. The tail is a brilliant fire-orange. The western chuck has more than 50 scales around the mid-forelimb.

This brightly colored morph of chuckwalla is of very localized distribution.

The Glen Canyon chuckwalla (*S. o. multiforaminatus*) has the smallest range of the four subspecies. It is found in a narrow diagonal along the Colorado River from Garfield County, Utah to the Glen Canyon Dam in north central Coconino County, Arizona. The banded immatures of this race are often clad in scales of brick-red. The bands, although obscuring somewhat with growth and age, are often visible throughout the life of the lizard, remaining better defined on the female.

The Peninsula chuckwalla (*S. obesus australis*) is rather similar to the western chuckwalla in appearance. The dorsal bands of this species have light centers and dark borders, thus appearing as double bands. There are more than 151 rows of ventral scales. It ranges southward in the western Baja from central Baja California Norte to the La Paz area of Baja California Sur.

The variable chuckwalla (*S. varius*) is both large and attractive. Its straw-tan ground cover is overlaid with variably sized and positioned patches of dark pigment. Some specimens are quite dark in overall color, but on most it is the light that prevails. Varius is found only on Isla San Esteban in the Gulf of California. The Arizona-Sonora Desert Museum (ASDM) in Tucson has researched this species extensively. Currently they have numerous individuals and have successfully bred them.

The rough-necked chuckwalla (*S. hispidus*) is large and of nearly an overall black in coloration. The head and nape scales are enlarged and tuberculate. This is an impressive species that the Arizona-Sonora Desert Museum once worked successfully with. However, a few years ago the ASDM chose to discontinue the breeding project with *hispidus* and channel all efforts into their program with *S. varius*. The rough-necked chuckwalla is restricted in range to Isla Angel de la Guarda and surrounding small islands located in the Gulf of California.

S. sleveni, a species with no common name, is restricted in distribution to the islands of Carmen, Coronados and

Monserrate in the Gulf of California. Like *hispidus*, *sleveni* is a dark species, but is of less rugose scalation. It, like the next species, is virtually unknown in American herpetoculture.

Like *S. sleveni*, *S. ater* has no common name. The latter occurs on the Gulf of California Islands of Espirutu Santo, San Francisco, Santa Cruz, San Marcos, San Diego, and Isla Partida. It is a banded species that most nearly resembles Baja's *S. australis* in both color and pattern.

Because Mexico protects all of its reptiles and amphibians and is reluctant to issue export permits to any but bona fide zoological research facilities, Mexican *Sauromalus* species are very rarely encountered. However, the American *S. obesus* is still rather generally available to hobbyists.

Given low humidity, high temperatures, spacious quarters, and suitable diet, chuckwallas can and do thrive as captives. They are ideal species for advanced hobbyists and zoological institutions.

In the wild the range of the common chuckwalla (*S. obesus* ssp.) is roughly similar to the range of the creosote bush. Besides the leaves of this desert plant, chucks consume considerable amounts of other vegetation; the flowers, leaves, and seeds of many desert annuals and perennials being included. Some insects are also consumed.

Chucks are oviparous lizards, the females laying a single clutch consisting of from a few to nearly a dozen large eggs. It is conjectured that many wild females produce their clutches only every second year. Captive females, traditionally better fed and having a somewhat longer annual activity period, may produce annually.

Chuckwallas have a relatively short annual activity period. As would be expected from a large lizard in a temperate climate, they emerge from hibernation rather late in the year (mid- to late April, depending on temperature) and retire again well before the cold weather has truly set in. Although "up and about" chucks are active only during the warmest part of the day. A body temperature of from 99 to 102°F (37.2–38.9°C) seems to be their operating optimum. At that temperature, for a big, heavy lizard, they are active, alert, wary, and even somewhat agile.

The Desert Iguana

It is from its generic name of "Dipsosaurus" that the vernacular of "dipso" comes for this little lizard. It is more commonly known as the "desert iguana."

The range of the desert iguana also follows that of the creosote bush closely and virtually parallels that of the chuckwalla. In fact, the leaves and blossoms of this desert shrub form the principal food of the desert iguana.

As with the chuckwallas, controversy surrounds not only the exact degree of dipso speciation but the subspeciation of *D. dorsalis* as well. Although some authorities feel there are as many as three species and that *dorsalis* contains three subspecies, other authorities feel that there is but the single species with no subspecies. The latter trend now seems most prevalent.

I had seen several desert iguanas on earlier trips. Most of them had appeared as tan "zipppps" as they sped across the Ajo Road in Pima County, Arizona. However, on each trip, we had always found the one or two specimens that hadn't safely made the dash. Even reduced to a two-dimensional road casualty from a vital desert being, the little lizards were beautiful creatures.

As Tom Tyning and I had proceeded deeply into Organ Pipe National Monument, we had seen more desert iguanas than ever before. But it was not until we got to the dune country of Imperial and San Diego Counties, California that we came to realize exactly how numerous these iguanids truly were.

There, while Tom and I searched for other species, desert iguanas were everywhere. They darted along roadways, they basked in the tracery of shadows beneath leafless desert shrubs, and they scurried into both isolated holes (probably of their own making, because desert iguanas are accomplished burrowers) and into the entrances of kangaroo rat middens at our approach. Some even clambered about (not awfully gracefully, I might add), well up in the creosote bushes, stopping now and again to consume a blossom or to taste new growth. When we would approach these arboreal lizards, they would "thump" heavily to the sand below and take off on a dead run toward their burrow. In those sandy, superheated, sparsely vegetated expanses, desert iguanas were abundant.

The desert iguana is an attractive lizard. Although heavy-bodied, it is not obesely so. It has a short head with a rounded snout, stout limbs, and a tapering tail that is about equal in length to that of the head and body. Except for the low vertebral crest, the body scales are small, whereas those of the tail are large and arranged in prominent whorls.

Although the ground color of *Dipsosaurus* varies somewhat (approximating the color of the sand in any given area), they always impart the appearance of a foot-long, tan lizard. The ground color is sandy gray and overlaid on the sides with a blush of brown or brownish red. Light ocelli are present anteriorly, wavy lines posteriorly.

Given ample warmth, low humidity, brightly lit, UV enhanced facilities,

Collecting and Keeping Native Lizard Species

Although there are no state or federal laws governing the collecting or keeping of the introduced green and spiny-tailed iguanas, this is not the case with the chuckwalla and desert iguana.

Laws regulating the taking and keeping of both species are in effect in several of the states in which these lizards are found. Should a specimen be carried interstate after being taken in violation of state laws, it becomes a federal offense as well.

To assure the legality of your pursuit we suggest that you check with the non-game division of your game and fish department *prior* to field collecting or even purchasing any of our native lizard species.

If you do acquire new specimens, they should be quarantined for a minimum of 30 days prior to bringing them in contact with the rest of your collection. During this quarantine period, it is suggested that a qualified veterinarian run fecal exams to ascertain that no communicable internal parasites are present. If parasites are present, they should be eliminated before placing the specimen with already established animals.

and a suitable diet, desert iguanas will thrive as captives. Some have neared the decade and a half mark, and there is little reason to believe that as we learn more about these lizards a time span of twenty years (or more) cannot be attained. Much remains to be learned about the breeding biology of these interesting arid-land lizards.

Desert iguanas are a small, beautiful and alert species native to southwestern United States and northwestern Mexico.

Photographing Iguanas

Once you've started keeping green iguanas, and then moved to observing their behavior in the wild, you may wish to move on to a new challenge: photography. Capturing an iguana on film combines husbandry and observation skills with the discipline necessary for picture taking. Each photo helps you to see how the next could be improved. Getting started is easy.

The equipment required will depend upon a number of variables. Among these are whether you will be taking photos of large lizards or small lizards, whether the photos will be of captives, staged, or in the wild and whether or not you are willing to devote to the hobby the time necessary to be successful. Of course, photographing captive or staged lizards is infinitely easier than pursuing and photographing free-ranging ones, but not nearly as satisfying.

Basic Equipment Needs

A sturdy 35-mm camera body with interchangeable lenses is suggested. You don't necessarily need a brand-new camera body and lenses; I've used quality secondhand equipment for many of my photographic ventures. You do need a photo supply dealer who can advise about the condition of the equipment you're buying, and who can tell you about some features of that particular lens or body (usually speaking, secondhand camera equipment does not come with manuals of any sort).

Lenses: The lenses I use include:
- a 28-mm wide angle for habitat photos
- a 50-mm standard for habitat photos
- a 100-mm macro for close-ups (suitable for almost every purpose)
- a 75–205-mm zoom lens for variable fieldwork
- a 400-mm fixed focal length telephoto lens for fieldwork
- a 120–600 zoom lens for distant but variable fieldwork

Strobes: a series of dedicated strobes (a dedicated strobe interfaces with the camera f-stop setting to furnish appropriate light levels).

Lens adapter: an ×1.25 to ×2 power lens adapter.

Film: ISO 50 slide film is slower, hence less "grainy" than the faster films often used for other purposes. This slower film will give you the best results, but also requires a bright day or electronic flashes to compensate for the slow speed. The higher the ISO, the less light you will need to photograph, but the "grainier" your pictures will be. If you are taking pictures with the hopes of having them published, use ISO 50 slide film. If you are taking photos merely for your own enjoyment, use either slide or print film, as you prefer.

Tripod: A sturdy tripod (an absolute necessity for the telephoto lenses) will hold your camera steady while you squeeze off that "once-in-a-lifetime" shot. Camera equipment with lenses is heavy, especially if you're out in the field and have slogged through hip-deep water and then scaled a couple of hillsides. The equipment is heavy even if you're indoors.

Camera body: After having a camera body malfunction, I now always have at least one spare body available.

A simple photographic stage can be built "on the spot" with tree limbs, bark or stone.

Some Photographic Hints

For staged photography, create a small natural setting by placing rocks, mosses, leaves, or bark—whichever is most appropriate for the species you're photographing—on a stage. In the past, I used a small lazy Susan as a stage, thinking I could rotate the stage with the animal on it, for different photographic angles. This works, providing that you move *very slowly*, both in your own actions and in rotating the stage. If you don't have a lazy Susan, just arrange the setting items on a tabletop or on a tree stump (outdoors or indoors, depending on where you are at the time), place the lizard, focus, and shoot. Having another person standing by to catch the iguana as it tries to run, will help.

Generally, if you don't spook the lizard, it will pause long enough in place to permit you to get a few shots.

You'll need to move quickly to capture the iguana when it moves, replace it on the stage, then move slowly to focus and shoot.

I created a backing for my stage with the top half of a round trash or garbage can, sectioned to size and then bolted into place just inside the edge rim of the lazy Susan. Black velvet clipped into place around the inside surface gives a good background for the lizard shots.

If you're trying field photography, approach the animal slowly and obliquely. Avoid eye contact. If the lizard notices you (of course it will!) freeze for a moment, then begin moving again. In some cases, you may need to approach as closely as possible in a car. I've taken many photos from inside my car, not because of comfort, but because as soon as I opened the car door, the lizards were gone.

A portable photo stage with a background can be easily made. In the field, camera-activated strobes will replace fixed lighting.

The Iguanidae:
A Family Portrait

The common green iguana and its close relatives are members of the lizard family Iguanidae. Iguanidae was once the catchall of lizard families. Iguanidae was one of the largest artificial assemblages of lizards, containing everything from anoles to basilisks to horned lizards to swifts. The shapes, sizes, and characteristics of those assembled species was amazing.

The recent reevaluation of the Iguanidae assemblage has dramatically decreased the number of species within the family. Now Iguanidae contains only a few genera of lizards. Among these are the namesake species, *Iguana iguana*, perhaps the most charming and popular of all lizards. Besides the familiar green iguanas, the family includes the spiny-tailed iguanas, Fijian iguanas, Galapagos iguanas, West Indian iguanas, desert iguanas, and chuckwallas.

These last six genera may not be as familiar to you as the ubiquitous green iguana, but that's because comparatively speaking, they're rarer than the green iguana. Indeed, several are threatened with extinction and may be seen only in the wild, at a zoo, or in the preserved collections at larger universities. The few specimens occasionally available are the result of captive-breeding programs or long-term captives that have been in private hands.

Most of the imperiled forms are insular species (island dwellers), and the status of their habitat is nearly as precarious as that of the lizards themselves. Islands, particularly those in subtropical or tropical areas, do not remain unpopulated by human beings for long. Human beings tend to take over any environment and those animals already in residence may be squeezed out, eaten, or stuffed and placed on varnished plaques and sold as curios.

Those iguanids in most serious trouble are the Galapagos, Fijian, most of the West Indian iguanas, and the chuckwallas found on tiny island groups in Mexico's Gulf of California. Laws and penalties are in place banning the capture or export of most of these imperiled species, but island development is hard to stop.

In contrast to their insular relatives, some of the mainland iguana species remain common enough to be mainstays of the pet industry. But even these species are no longer indiscriminately collected or exported. The better-known examples are the green iguana of South America, the desert iguana of the southwestern United States and the mainland chuckwalla of the southwestern United States and northern Mexico.

Certain of the iguanids have been introduced and have become established in areas far distant from their normal ranges. For instance, the green iguana (*Iguana iguana*) is now well established in Hawaii and southern Florida and the Mexican spiny-tailed iguana (*Ctenosaura pectinata*) is present in many areas of the lower Rio Grande Valley, near Tucson, Arizona, and in parts of Florida.

Advisement

Illegal dealing, either purposely or in ignorance, in endangered or threatened species (whether the species is reptile, mammal, or insect), is considered a serious offense. The penalties include very large fines and may involve jail sentences as well.

Permitation must be procured prior to the interstate purchase and transportation, importing, or exporting, of any endangered or threatened wildlife. This includes specimens otherwise legally held and captive-bred. Most insular iguanas fall into this category.

In the United States, contact the Fish and Wildlife Service as to the current status of an iguana species. Look in the yellow pages of your telephone book under U.S. Government. Do not expect the person answering the phone to be an expert in the status of lizards; you'll be referred to a USF&W agent.

It is both illegal and immoral to turn exotic species loose outside of their natural ranges. Some exotics may have considerable adverse impact on native species if they do become established.

Many of the impressive iguanids mentioned here have no common English names. In an effort to promote uniformity, I have, herein, often used names recently coined by David Blair and Robert Ehrig, two foremost breeders of rare iguanas. Other names are those that appear in Frank Slavens' *Reptiles and Amphibians in Captivity*. (This book is also the source from which the zoo status mentioned in the following accounts has been adapted.)

Here are some notes on the iguanas of the world, including ranges, population status (when known), and zoos in which they may be seen.

Key:
(E)   species listed as endangered
(T)   species considered threatened
(NL)   species not listed as either threatened or endangered
(X)   indicates an (probable) extinct form

Species Accounts:

Iguana iguana;
Common Green Iguana (NL)

This is the most widely ranging iguanid. It occurs naturally from northern Mexico to southern Brazil and westward to Paraguay. It is found naturally on some islands of the Lesser Antilles, has been introduced and established on others, and is also present in breeding colonies in Florida and Hawaii. It may also be established in Cameron County, Texas, in the Lower Rio Grande Valley. Adult males occasionally exceed 6 feet (1.8 m) in length.

This species is present in nearly every zoological garden and in thousands of private homes and pet shops across the world.

The green iguana, Iguana iguana.

Iguana delicatissima;
Antillean Green Iguana (NL)

Unfortunately, this species seem to now be losing ground because of habitat degradation and serious competition from the introduced common green iguana. The historic range included many of the islands of the Lesser Antilles. This species nears 6 feet (1.8 m) in length.

Only the Memphis Zoo reports this species in its collection.

Other iguana genera:

Amblyrhynchus cristatus ssp.;
Galapagos Marine Iguana (NL)

(Several rather poorly defined subspecies exist, each on a different island in the Galapagos Archipiélago.)

The adult size varies considerably, the largest specimens attaining an overall length of more than 5 feet (1.5 m).

The various races of this species comprise the world's only exclusively marine lizard. They crop marine alga from rocks, diving and submerging in rather turbulent waters to do so. The short snout and powerful jaws are well adapted for such foraging, allowing the lizards ample leverage to remove these simple plants from their holdtights. A salt gland excretes the salt through the nostrils. This species has long been protected over its entire range. The dietary necessities would make them poor candidates for successful captive husbandry even if not protected. None are currently captive in either private or public collections in the United States.

Brachylophus fasciatus;
Fiji Banded Iguana (E)

This beautiful blue-banded green iguana (males only, females are entirely green) is classified as an endangered species, hence entirely protected from harassment and exploitation. Several captive breeding

The marine iguana, Amblyrhynchus cristatus.

programs are in place in United States and European zoos.

This species is one of a mere handful of Pacific Island iguanas. Males slightly exceed 2.5 feet (0.8 m) in overall length; females are somewhat smaller. Males have a low serrate crest. This species occurs on Fiji and Tonga, or in the United States at the Cincinnati, Dallas, Fresno, and San Diego zoos.

Brachylophus fasciatus, the Fiji iguana.

75

Brachylophus vitiensis; Fiji Crested Iguana (E)

This species is quite similar in appearance to the Fiji Banded Iguana, but has a proportionately higher crest. This is especially evident in the nuchal (nape) area. The Fiji Crested Iguana is restricted in distribution to Fiji.

No individuals of this species are reported as being in zoological gardens.

Conolophus pallidus; Galapagos Land Iguana (E)

Whether there is one or two species of these impressive lizards will depend on the authority quoted. They are restricted in distribution to Ecuador's Galapagos Islands. Adults attain 3.5 feet (1.1 m) in overall length. (This species may be identical to the *Conolophus subcristata*.)

Reportedly, no Galapagos Land iguanas of either species are in zoological collections.

Conolophus subcristata; Galapagos Land Iguana (E)

Considered by some authorities the sole species of land-dwelling iguana of the Galapagos Islands.

The Yucatan dwarf spiny-tailed iguana, Ctenosaura defensor.

Ctenosaura acanthura; Spiny-tailed Iguana (NL)

This is the large spiny-tail of Mexico's Gulf Coast. It remains abundant throughout its range. Adult size is in excess of 3 feet (0.9 m).

Although a few of these lizards are present in private breeding collections, none are reported in the collections of public zoological gardens.

Ctenosaura bakeri; Isla de la Bahia Spiny-tailed Iguana (NL)

Little has been published about this form which is restricted in distribution to Isla de la Bahia, Honduras.

No *C. bakeri* are in zoos.

Ctenosaura (Enyliosaurus) clarki; Michoacan (Clark's) Dwarf Spiny-tailed Iguana (NL)

Less colorful than the closely allied Yucatan spiny-tail, Clark's spiny-tail occurs on the Pacific coast of central Mexico. Because Mexico now protects and prohibits export (except under scientific permit) of all wildlife, *C. clarki* is seldom seen in the United States. However, the Texas Fort Worth Zoo reports having three specimens in their collection.

Ctenosaura (Enyliosaurus) defensor; Yucatan Dwarf Spiny-tailed Iguana (NL)

This is one of the smallest and most colorful of the spiny-tailed iguanas. They are particularly common on the Yucatan Peninsula. Adult males attain a length of about 10 inches (25.4 cm); females are smaller.

No zoological gardens are reported as having this pretty little iguana on display.

Ctenosaura hemilopha; Sonoran Spiny-tailed Iguana (NL)

This is one of the large ctenosaurs. A large, dark lizard, the Sonoran spiny-tail is widely distributed in

Mexico's northern Pacific states and in eastern and southern Baja California Sur. The tail involves more than one half of the 30-inch (76.2 cm) overall length.

Both the Detroit Zoo and the Arizona-Sonora Desert Museum (Tucson, Arizona) have specimens on exhibit.

Ctenosaura oeirhina;
Roatan Island Spiny-tailed Iguana (NL)

This is another species with a very restricted distribution. It occurs only on Roatan Island, Honduras. Little is known with certainty about this species.

None are present in zoos.

Ctenosaura (Enyliosaurus) palearis;
Central American (Honduran) Dwarf Spiny-tailed Iguana (NL)

This species is an inhabitant of the semiarid lowlands of Guatemala and Honduras. Large males may attain a 15-inch (38.1 cm) overall length. Females are smaller.

Woodland Park Zoo (Seattle, Washington) reports having this species on display.

Ctenosaura pectinata;
Mexican Spiny-tailed Iguana (NL)

With adult males occasionally attaining an overall length of nearly 4 feet (1.2 m), this is one of the largest of the spiny-tails. Although the natural range is from Sinaloa to Oaxaca along Mexico's Pacific coast, populations are now established in Dade and Charlotte counties, Florida and the Lower Rio Grande Valley of Texas (Cameron and Hidalgo counties). This is an abundant species.

This species may be seen in the collections of the Indianapolis, Los Angeles, Philadelphia, and Staten Island zoos. It is also the common spiny-tail of the pet trade.

The Central American dwarf spiny-tailed iguana, Ctenosaura palearis.

Ctenosaura (Enyliosaurus) quinquecarinata;
Dwarf Spiny-tailed Iguana (NL)

Although this species is frequently referred to in the pet trade as the "Nicaraguan spiny-tailed" (or "club-tailed" iguana, its actual range is from the Isthmus of Tehuantepic in Mexico's state of Oaxaca southward

The Mexican spiny-tailed iguana, Ctenosaura pectinata.

The dwarf spiny-tailed iguana, Ctenosaura quinquecarinata.

to Nicaragua. One of the larger of the dwarf forms, this species attains an overall length of about 17 inches (43.2 cm).

This species has only recently begun appearing in the American and European pet trades.

Ctenosaura similis;
Spiny-tailed Iguana (NL)

This is another of the larger spiny-tails. It is common to abundant throughout much of southern Mexico from the

The spiny-tailed iguana, Ctenosaura similis.

northernmost areas of the Yucatan Peninsula southward to Panama.

Columbus (Ohio) and Dallas zoos have this species on display.

Cyclura carinata bartschi;
Booby Cay (Bartschi's)
Rock Iguana (T)

In keeping with many other species of rock iguanas, males of this species are considerably larger than the females. Males may attain a snout-vent length of about 13 inches (33 cm), total length of slightly more than two feet (0.6 m). Females are several inches smaller. Fewer than 300 of this small rock iguana are thought to remain on its home island, Booby Cay, Bahama Islands. It is considered a threatened species. It is certainly a vulnerable species.

None are reported in the collections of public zoos.

Cyclura carinata carinata;
Turks and Caicos Rock Iguana (T)

This is a slightly larger subspecies of *Cyclura carinata*. Males attain an overall length of about 15 inches. Total length is about twice that. Females are a few inches smaller. It is thought that about 10,000 specimens remain on the Turks and Caicos Islands. Despite this not inconsiderable number, Turks and Caicos iguanas are vulnerable to both habitat degradation and human exploitation.

None are reported in zoo collections.

Cyclura collei;
Jamaican Rock Iguana (E)

One of the most critically endangered of the rock iguanas, this species was thought for many years to actually be extinct. Elated researchers rediscovered the species in 1990. Although unquestionably extant, it is thought that fewer than 100 specimens survive, and these only in the remote Hellshire Hills of

Jamaica. Males of this species may near, or even slightly exceed, 3.5 feet (1.1 m) in overall length. Females are somewhat smaller.

Although the Ft. Worth (Texas) Zoo is helping to spearhead conservation efforts for this species, none are reported in captivity other than at a research facility in Jamaica.

Cyclura cornuta cornuta; Hispaniolan Rhinoceros Iguana (NL)

This is not only one of the largest and most impressive of the rock iguanas, but remains one of the more common as well. Population estimates are difficult to make with any degree of accuracy on an island as large, topographically diverse, and inhospitable as Hispaniola, but there are perhaps 10,000 individuals of this big lizard left in the wild. This is the rock iguana most frequently seen in captivity in U.S. facilities. It is one of the few not regulated in trade in the United States by the U.S. Endangered Species Act as well.

Adult male Hispaniolan rhinoceros iguanas attain massive proportions. They not only attain a total length of nearly 4 feet (1.2 m) (of which about half is tail) but are correspondingly heavy bodied as well. A weight of 15 pounds (6.8 kg) is attained by some. Old males develop massive heads with greatly enlarged, rounded, temporal areas and pronounced, broadly conical nasal horns (from which both common and scientific names are derived). Although the females are smaller and less proportionately heavy, their nasal horns may be proportionately longer than those of the males.

A great many zoos have rhinoceros iguanas on display. Among other facilities these impressive animals may be seen at the Atlanta, Bronx, Brookfield (Illinois), Dallas, El Paso, Fort Worth, Gladys Porter (Brownsville, Texas), Houston, Indianapolis, Lincoln Park (Chicago, Illinois), Louisville,

The Hispaniolan rhinoceros iguana, Cyclura c. cornuta.

Sedgewick County (Wichita, Kansas), Staten Island (New York), and National (Washington, D.C.) zoos.

Cyclura cornuta onchioppsis; Navassa Island Rhinoceros Iguana (X)

A somewhat smaller form of rhinoceros iguana, the Navassa Island rhino is now thought to be extinct. It was restricted in distribution to the island from which it takes its name.

Cyclura cornuta stejnegeri; Mona Island Rhinoceros Iguana (T)

As large as the nominate form, the Mona Island rhinoceros iguana is restricted in distribution to tiny Isla Mona, east of Puerto Rico. A population of about 3,000 is estimated to remain.

Only the San Diego Zoo reports having this species in their collections.

Cyclura cychlura cychlura; Andros Island Rock Iguana (T)

This rock iguana, which attains an overall length of about 34 inches (86.4 cm), is restricted in distribution to Andros Island in the Bahama Islands. The females attain nearly as great a size as the males. It is possible that as many as 5,000 Andros Island rock iguanas remain in the wild.

No zoos report having the various subspecies of *C. cychlura* in their collections.

Cyclura cychlura figginsi; Exuma Island Rock Iguana (T)

This subspecies exists in small numbers on the central and southern Exuma Cays, Bahama Islands. It is a threatened subspecies and probably fewer than 1,000 exist. This sub-species is smaller than the nominate form, attaining an overall length of about 30 inches (76.2 cm). Of this length, about half is tail. It is thought that the total population of this race is less than 1,000 individuals.

Cyclura cychlura inornata; Allen's Cay Rock Iguana (T)

This 32-inch (81.3 cm) long sub-species is a member of the herpeto-fauna of the Northern Exuma Cays, Bahama Islands. This race is interme-diate in size between the Andros and southern Exuma races. Probably fewer than 500 exist.

Allen's cay rock iguana, Cyclura cychlura inornata.

Cyclura nubila caymanensis; Cayman Island Rock Iguana (T)

Although originally restricted to Little Cayman Island and Cayman Brac, this race has now been introduced to Grand Cayman Island where it inter-grades with the more seriously imper-iled Grand Cayman blue rock iguana. A total length of slightly less than 40 inches (101.6 cm) is attained by adult males. Females are a few inches smaller. Perhaps 1,000 individuals of this race remain.

A specimen at the Atlanta Zoo is probably of this race.

Cyclura nubila lewisi, Grand Cayman Blue Rock Iguana (E)

Until recently it was estimated that about 250 individuals of this endan-gered race remained alive in the more inaccessible regions of Grand Cayman Island. However, it has recently been determined that the introduced Cayman Island rock iguana has intergraded with these slightly larger and more seriously endangered cousins. It is now thought that fewer than 75 pure-blooded Grand Cayman blue rock iguanas exist.

The Cayman island rock iguana, Cyclura nubila caymenensis.

Efforts are being made to maintain the pure lineage through captive breeding projects on Grand Cayman Island and at the following zoological gardens: Central Florida (Lake Monroe, Florida), Indianapolis (Indiana), San Antonio (Texas), and San Diego (California).

Cyclura nubila nubila, Cuban Rock Iguana (T: Cuban population; NL: Puerto Rican population)

This is both the largest and most secure of the three races of *C. nubila*. It is thought that up to 10,000 exist in the natural population on Cuba and the introduced population on Isla Mayaguez, Puerto Rico. The legal status of this animal is complicated. Whereas the Cuban populations are considered threatened, requiring federal permits for interstate movement, the unprotected Puerto Rican population requires no such documentation. DNA sequencing can accurately identify the origin of the specimen(s) in question. This is the largest of the rock iguanas, adult males occasionally attaining or even slightly exceeding a full 5 feet (1.5 m) in length. Although smaller, the females attain a respectable 4.5 feet (1.4 m) in overall length.

The Indianapolis (Indiana), Memphis (Tennessee), and Milwaukee (Wisconsin) zoos report this species in their collections.

Cyclura pinguis; Anegada Island Rock Iguana (E)

It is thought that fewer than 1,500 of these impressive 45-inch (114.3 cm) long iguanas remain alive. They are restricted in distribution to Anegada Island in the British Virgins. Females are somewhat smaller than the males.

None are reported in captivity.

Cyclura ricordi; Hispaniolan (or Ricord's) Rock Iguana (NL)

Only on the island of Hispaniola do two species of rock iguanas naturally

The Grand Cayman blue rock iguana, *Cyclura nubila lewisi*.

coexist. This species is somewhat smaller (adult males top out at about 35 inches [88.9 cm]) than the sympatric rhinoceros iguana. Although an accurate estimate of the population of Ricord's rock iguana has not been possible, it is conjectured that fewer than 2,500 remain.

The Indianapolis Zoo reports having three specimens on display.

A young specimen of the rhinoceros iguana Cyclura c. cornuta.

The Anegada island rock iguana, Cyclura pinguis.

Cyclura rileyi cristata; Sandy Cay Rock Iguana (T)

This 2-foot (0.6 m) rock iguana is restricted to a very few islands in the southern Exumas, but is not sympatric with *C. cychlura*. Perhaps as few as 250 specimens remain alive.

None of the various races of *C. rileyi* are reported captive.

Cyclura rileyi nuchalis; Crooked-Acklins Island Rock Iguana (T)

Although solidly built, even the largest males of this diminutive rock iguana seldom exceed 22 inches (55.9 cm) in overall length. The females are smaller. The 500 or fewer remaining specimens are restricted to Cays in the Bight of Acklins, Southern Exuma Cays, Bahama Islands.

Cyclura rileyi rileyi; San Salvador Rock Iguana (E)

Another diminutive race, this husky little rock iguana tops out at somewhat less than a 2-foot (0.6 m) overall length. It is restricted to the Cay of San Salvador in the southern Exuma Islands of the Bahamas. Estimates of the numbers remaining vary from 500 individuals to three times that number.

Dipsosaurus dorsalis; Desert Iguana (NL)

Whether or not subspecies exist in this 13 inch (30.5 cm) long lizard species is conjectural. The current trend, echoed herein, is to consider both the genus and the species monotypic. Although populations are suppressed by habitat degradation in some areas, in others this diminutive iguanid remains one of the most common of lizard species. It may be found southward from the southwestern United States (Arizona, California, Nevada, and extreme southwestern Utah), southward along the entire length of Mexico's Baja Peninsula (including many islands and islets) and eastward throughout most of Sonora and northwestern Sinaloa.

A great many zoos display this little iguana. Among them are Arizona-Sonora Desert Museum (Tucson, Arizona), Honolulu, Houston, Indianapolis, John Ball Zoo (Grand Rapids, Michigan), Lincoln Park (Chicago, Illinois), Los Angeles (California), Louisville (Kentucky), National (Washington, D.C.), Oklahoma City, Riverside (Columbia, South Carolina), Roger Williams (Providence, Rhode Island), and Tulsa (Oklahoma).

Sauromalus ater ater; Chuckwalla (NL)

This species is restricted in distribution to the Mexican Islands of Espiritu Santo, San Francisco, San Jose, Santa Cruz, San Diego and Isla Partida in the Gulf of California. Large males attain more than 16 inches (40.6 cm). Females are smaller.

No zoological facility has listed any race of this species in their present collections.

Sauromalus ater klauberi; Chuckwalla (NL)

This race is known only from Santa Catalina Island in the Gulf of California.

SaEuromalus ater shawi;
Chuckwalla (NL)

This Mexican rarity is restricted to Isla San Marcos in Mexico's Gulf of California.

Sauromalus australis;
Baja Peninsula Chuckwalla (NL)

This species is found in southeastern Baja California Norte and most of eastern Baja California Sur, south to La Paz. Considered a subspecies of *S. obesus* by some authorities, momentum to consider the animal a full species is now picking up. Adult males may occasionally exceed 16 inches (40.6 cm). Females are smaller.

There are apparently no Baja Peninsula chuckwallas captive in public collections.

Sauromalus hispidus;
Black (Rough-Scaled) Chuckwalla (NL)

This is another insular form from Mexico's Gulf of California. It occurs only on the island of Angel de la Guarda and its surrounding satellites. This species nears 2 feet (0.6 m) in length.

Several facilities list this species in their collections. Among others are the Arizona-Sonora Desert Museum (Tucson) and the Fort Worth (Texas) Zoo.

Sauromalus obesus multiforminatus; Glen Canyon Chuckwalla (NL)

· This subspecies occurs in a narrow diagonal along the Colorado River from Garfield County, Utah to the Glen Canyon Dam in northern central Coconino County, Arizona. Large males of all races may exceed 16 inches (40.6 cm). Females are smaller.

Nearly every large zoo has a common chuckwalla of some subspecies in their public collections.

The desert iguana, Dipsosaurus dorsalis.

Sauromalus obesus obesus;
Western Chuckwalla (NL)

This widespread and rather common lizard is found in suitable rocky habitats from southwestern Utah westward across Nevada to eastern central California, then southward through all of western Arizona and the northern Baja Peninsula.

The black chuckwalla, Sauromalus hispidus.

The western chuckwalla, Sauromalus o. obesus.

Sauromalus obesus townsendi; Sonoran Desert Chuckwalla (NL)

This race is found only in the western sections of the Mexican state of Sonora and on a very few of the islands that lie just off of the coast in the eastern Gulf of California.

Sauromalus obesus tumidus; Arizona Chuckwalla (NL)

This is the chuckwalla seen in central and extreme southwestern Arizona

and southwestern Sonora, Mexico. It is attractive and abundant in suitably rocky habitats.

Sauromalus sleveni; Chuckwalla (NL)

Another on the western Gulf of California insular forms, *S. sleveni* is restricted in distribution to Islas Carmen, Coronados, and Monserrate. It is seldom seen. Adult males near 18 inches (45.7 cm) in length.

No public facility has listed this species as being currently in their collections.

Sauromalus varius; San Esteban (Painted) Chuckwalla (E)

The largest of the chuckwallas, *S. varius* occasionally attains a 2-foot (0.6 m) overall length. It is restricted in distribution to Mexico's Islas San Esteban, Lobos, and Pelicano in the western Gulf of California.

Several facilities are working with this impressive chuckwalla. Among these are the Arizona-Sonora Desert Museum (Tucson, Arizona), Houston Zoo, Louisville Zoo, and the Rio Grande Zoo (Albuquerque, New Mexico).

The Arizona chuckwalla, Sauromalus obesus tumidus.

Useful Literature and Addresses

You can find other hobbyists through your local pet store, library, university, or community college, or "on-line" via Internet, Compuserve, and Herp-Net.

Herpetological Societies

The International Iguana Society (IIS) (Rte 3, Box 328, Big Pine Key, Florida 33043) is a nonprofit corporation dedicated to the conservation, biological diversity, and herpetoculture of the iguanas of the world. A quarterly newsletter, the *Iguana Times*, is sent to members.

Herpetological societies also exist in many larger cities. Periodically updated listings of existing societies are often carried as a public service by the national magazines dedicated to the field of herpetology and herpetoculture.

Magazines and Journals

The following magazines are just a few examples of the periodicals available through subscription, pet shops, or on newsstands:

Reptile and Amphibian
An excellent small format journal currently produced bimonthly. Subscriptions are available from *Reptile and Amphibian* RD3, Box 3709-A, Pottsville, Pennsylvania 17901.

Reptiles
A larger format magazine dedicated primarily to herpetoculture and conservation, currently bimonthly but scheduled to soon become a monthly. Subscription information may be obtained from *Reptiles* Magazine, P.O. Box 6050, Mission Viejo, California 92690-6050.

The Vivarium
The publication of the American Federation of Herpetoculturists (AFH), bimonthly and of large format. It is available by membership in the AFH, P.O. Box 300067, Escondido, CA 92030-0067.

Herp Review and the *Journal of Herpetology*
The Society for the Study of Reptiles and Amphibians (SSRA) publishes a nontechnical periodical, *Herp Review*, and the more scholarly, *Journal of Herpetology*. Subscriptions are available from SSRA, Department of Zoology, Miami University, Oxford, Ohio 45056.

Copeia
The American Society of Ichthyologists and Herpetologists (ASIH) publishes *Copeia*, a technical journal that includes reptiles, amphibians, and fish. Subscription information is available from ASIH, Department of Zoology, Southern Illinois University, Carbondale, Illinois 62901-6501.

Books

Burghardt, G.M. and A.S. Rand (Eds.) *Iguanas of the World: Their Behavior, Ecology, and Conservation*. Park Ridge, New Jersey: Noyes Publishing, 1982.
This very informative and scholarly volume, currently out of print, will soon be reissued by Krieger Publishing.

Frye, F.L. and W. Townsend. *Iguanas: A Guide to Their Biology and Captive Care.* Malabar, Florida: Krieger Publishing 1993.
An excellent, up-to-date compendium of information about the green iguana.

Stanoszewski, M. *The Manual of Lizards and Snakes.* Morris Plains, New Jersey: Tetra Press, 1990.
This is an excellent volume outlining the general husbandry techniques for a multitude of species.

Sources

If unavailable locally, you can buy prepared iguana diets from the following:

Pretty Pets
5810 Stacy Trail, P.O. Box 177
Stacy, MN 55079-0177
1-800-356-5020

Vite-A-Diet
D&P Enterprises
106 Township Square
Lawrenceburg, KY 40342
1-502-839-0876

Nutri-Grow Iguana Diet
118 South Main Street
Dry Ridge, KY 41035
606-824-9950

Glossary

aestivation a period of warm weather inactivity. It is the summertime equivalent of hibernation.

allopatric not occurring together but often adjacent

ambient temperature the temperature of the environment

anterior toward the front

arboreal tree-dwelling

attenuated long and slender, as a iguana's original tail

autotomize the ability to break easily or voluntarily cast off a part of the body.

brumation the reptilian and amphibian equivalent of mammalian hibernation

caudal pertaining to the tail

cloaca the common chamber into which digestive, urinary and reproductive systems empty and that opens exteriorly through the vent or anus

crepuscular active at dusk or dawn

crest a ridge, usually of enlarged or attenuated scales along the nape, back, and/or basal tail area of an iguana

deposition the laying of eggs

deposition site spot chosen by the female to lay eggs.

dichromatic two color phases of the same species

dimorphic a difference in form, build, or coloration involving the same species

diurnal active in the daytime

dorsal pertaining to the back; upper surface

dorsum the upper surface

endemic confined to a specific region

femoral pores openings on the underside of the thighs of lizards; they produce a waxy exudate

femur the part of the leg between hip and knee

form an identifiable species or subspecies

fracture planes softer areas in the tail vertebrae that allow the tail to break easily.

genus a group of species having similar characteristics.

granular pertaining to small, flat scales

gravid the reptilian equivalent of mammalian pregnancy

gular pertaining to the throat

heliothermic pertaining to a species that basks in the sun

hemipenes the dual copulatory organs of male lizards and snakes

hybrid offspring resulting from the breeding of two species

insular island-dwelling

intergrade offspring of the breeding of two subspecies

juvenile a young or immature specimen

keel a ridge (along the center of a scale)

labial pertaining to the lips

lateral pertaining to the side

melanism a profusion of black pigment

middorsal pertaining to the middle of the back

midventral pertaining to the center of the abdomen

monotypic having but one type

nocturnal active at night

ocelli dots or "eye spots" (often with a light colored center) on lizard's skin

oviparous reproducing with eggs that hatch after laying

ovoviviparous reproducing with shelled or membrane-contained eggs that hatch prior to, or at deposition

parietal eye a sensory organ positioned mid-cranially in certain reptiles

phalanges bones of the toes

poikilothermic a species with no internal body temperature regulation; "cold-blooded"

race a subspecies

rugose not smooth, wrinkled or tuberculate

saxicolous rock-dwelling

serrate sawlike

species a group of similar creatures that produce viable young when breeding.

subspecies the subdivision of a species. A race that may differ slightly in color, size, scalation, or other criteria.

sympatric occurring together

taxonomy the classification of plants and animals

terrestrial land-dwelling

thermoregulate to regulate (body) temperature by choosing a warmer or cooler environment

thigmothermic pertaining to a species (often nocturnal) that thermoregulates by being in contact with a preheated surface, such as a boulder

tubercles warty protuberances

tympanum the external eardrum

vent the external opening of the cloaca; the anus

venter the belly

ventral pertaining to the undersurface or belly

Index

Numerals in **bold face type** indicate color photos. **C1** indicates front cover; **C2**, inside front cover; **C3**, inside back cover; **C4**, back cover.